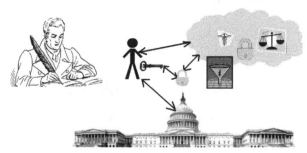

Government 2.0

Re Forming Government for the 21ˢᵗ Century

Volume 1 – Vision and Architecture

By

Stephen Imholt

ISBN-13: 978-0692458549

ISBN-10: 0692458549

For information address

Top Wing Books

3202 Woodrow Ave

Richmond VA 23222

DEDICATION

To my grandchildren, who just by being the delight that they are, convinced me of the need for this kind of a book.

To my daughter the doctor, who said you can't change medicine that way. To my daughter the teacher, who said you can't change education that way. To my daughter the lawyer who said you can't change the law that way. To my son the IT wunderkind who said, "You can't tell readers that way. You need to tell the reader what they need to hear in a way that will interest them."

To my best friend, my wife who said, "It will never happen because people are too complacent." And to friends who have said, it will never happen because people have become too despondent.

Each of whom made me work and rewrite, cogitate and regurgitate until they also said, "I'm tired of hearing about it, I'll read it when you are done." Some even admitted that "If it ever actually happened, it would be really good".

And thanks to Robert Heinlein, for TANSTAAFL (There Ain't No Such Thing As A Free Lunch).

FORWARD

There is a possible future where

- The government pays little attention to the law.
- Government actually serving the people is a myth.
- The individual has no ability to affect the operations of government.
- The individual cannot even hope to have an impact on how the government interacts with them.
- It is only a myth that you control the government.
- You know government is controlled by forces you can never begin to affect.
- The idea of government by the people means only the people who control the government.

Unfortunately, *that is* the future slowly growing in this country from the government of today to the government which is effectively an elected tyranny.

Or

There *can be* a future where

- The direction we have been going, is changed bit by bit, month by month, and year by year.
- You can actually control the federal government where it affects you most, at the local level.
- The government obviously works for you.
- You actually have a voice that can be heard.
- We together as one nation develop an improved way of doing things just we always have.
- We act to protect all of our rights together, including our electronic property, our identity.
- By the very design of our governmental services we are actually aided in protecting our rights.
- The government in the future will be closer to that ideal those past generations of Americans before us fought to keep from being lost.

Either future can happen. The question is which way will our country go?

The following examples show one way that this country could transform itself again.

Chuck Stewart's Medical Records[1]

Chuck gets an email on his cell phone from his physician about needing his annual checkup. The note includes a request to allow the physician to access Chuck's Personal Data Store (PDS). This is where Chuck's electronic medical record is stored. The note also includes a link to the physician's office schedule.

Going to his PDS on Amazon, Chuck accesses his electronic medical record (EMR) and sets up a temporary pass code. Then he uses the link to go to the physician's office schedule software. There he picks an appointment time which he does and provides the pass code so the physician can get into his EMR.

This gives the physician complete access to Chuck's EMR, and if Chuck needs a hospital, a specialist, or even just wants to change physicians, his information is always available under his control.

We can do everything in Chuck's story using technology we already have. However, we would need yet another change in the way we expect health care to work.

Next consider this story about the Schmidt family.

---

[1] All names in the stories in this book are fictitious.

Johan Schmidt and his Personal Data Store

Johan uses his Personal Data Store (PDS) from Hewlett Packard a lot. Since Johan lost his job a couple of months back, he hasn't been able to pay for his full PDS. Nevertheless, because the government pays for a limited PDS for those who can't pay, he can still access the government and medical wings in his PDS.

Johan has been making heavy use of his PDS to report to the State of Utah Department of Workforce Services (UTDWS) his effort to find work. He is required to do this each week. Because he reports his efforts this way, the UTDWS can directly deposit his weekly unemployment compensation payments.

Again, does this sound farfetched? From a technology standpoint, this is not only practical but also easy.

The next story is not so much about technology, but instead making real changes in how we interact with each other, supported by technology.

Jerry Smallwood gets an apartment in a new town

Jerry Smallwood is a college graduate who is moving to a new town to start his first job. Jerry tries to rent an apartment near his new employer. He is told by Fred the leasing agent that there are no apartments available. Later he finds out that there are open apartments. He goes ahead and rents one through Sally the complex manager. Jerry knows in his gut that Fred told him that there were no apartments because he is black.

Jerry had heard about the way the new Federal Neighborhood Offices (FNO) were able to follow up on discrimination cases quickly with actual resolution. Jerry thought he should check this out.

To make a long story short, within 30 days of Jerry filing the complaint, and after only one court hearing at the Federal Local Magistrate Court (FLMC), Fred had been found guilty and fined $250. Jerry also found out that if he had actually rented the apartment the fine would have been much higher. It helped that Sally, the complex manager, had submitted a statement on his NOT Fred's behalf. That made Jerry feel better too.

None of these things are beyond today except we haven't done them. How about a change to improve getting out the vote for everyone.

Will and Wanda Vogt and the election

Both Willa and Will are retired, and tend to lose track of the days. Will knows he can be forgetful, so he makes sure that his Calendar on his computer lets him know about important things he should do.

When Will checks he sees the reminder that today is Election Day. Because California uses the Federal Electronic Voting System (FEVS[2]), they can vote directly from home. So Will logs into the FEVS system from his PDS. The FEVS system automatically points him directly to California ballot appropriate to their location. The ballot not only has a spot to vote for the local public Waste Management Board but the new local Federal Neighborhood Office Board. After Will finishes voting, Willa logs in and votes as well.

If you think about it, technology can make government work much better if we take the time to actually design things better. This has the potential to both improve our government and to benefit to our society as a whole. The catch of course, is how do you do that and actually protect people's rights.

If you like the above examples, wait until you read the stories of how the IRS[i] could be changed.

Is this really a Possible Future?

---

2. This is the name assigned to a hypothetical federal law allowng electronic voting using secure software.

Yes it can be, either with the people controlling the government, or with the government more completely controlling the people with each passing year. It could happen. The question is which future do we want?

GENERAL NOTE

Some readers will only want to read a book because it has only a particular tilt in perspective. For example, some conservatives would only read Glenn Beck, while some liberals would only read someone like Ed Schulz. So you may want to know is this a liberal or conservative slanted book. The answer is yes, it is.

You may want to read the different viewpoints that are included in the Appendices under perspectives. It is suggested though, that you read Chapter 3 before reading the perspectives. That way you can get a clear understanding of what could be done. If you are looking for 30-second sound bites, this book is unlikely to interest you. If you want to get a clear understanding of what could be done if we properly employ technology to benefit the entire country, you probably should keep reading.

TABLE OF CONTENTS

INTRODUCTION

The US government is the first government that was actually designed.

Today we can look at the original Articles of Confederation, and see that it was full of gaps. It didn't really provide for a very good national government. You can think of the Confederation as US government 1.0.

The first version of US government was pretty bad just like the first version of most software products. There were actual rebellions and threats of rebellions during the years when the country was run as the Confederation. The Confederation had many problems which is why it lasted less than 10 years.

But the US Constitution which could be called government 1.5 has been a tremendous success. It's lasted over 200 years, and is still going. It's done so because originally it was very well architected.

In many ways, our Constitution is like well-designed software. It had clearly laid out the basic goals. Goals like to form a more perfect union, and to establish justice. Goals such as insure domestic tranquility and provide for the common defense. The Constitution even had the goals to promote the general welfare and secure the blessings of liberty to ourselves and our posterity.

Like all good systems, the basic design was clear and concise. The Constitution laid out 3 branches of government. It separated the power between those branches and the states. It set length of office for people in the government. It even said that there were limits on the scope of government.

When the Constitution was first approved by the States it had a good design. Over time most of the amendments improved the design of the government. There were a few amendments that were not so great in the overall design such as prohibition. And there were a few amendments that took a couple of tries to fix the basic problems of slavery. The Thirteenth amendment was first which outlawed slavery. Then the Fourteenth which was needed to insure that former slaves were recognized as citizens. And then there was the Fifteenth amendment which was needed to insure that these equal citizens actually had equality in voting. And lastly almost a century later, was the amendment which made it unconstitutional to charge a tax for the right to vote.

Over ten thousand proposals to amend the constitution have been proposed since it was first ratified. Less than fifty of these proposed amendments went to the states for ratification. And only twenty-seven have ever been ratified.

There is even a way to change the Constitution if needed where the states start the process. But that method has never actually been used, although it has been started a number of times.

To me, it is this ability to amend the design that is the most interesting piece of the entire Constitution.

The founding fathers were able to realize that the Constitution barely provided an outline to how the government would actually work, so they provided a way of changing the design *within* the design. In software design, the idea of self-correcting code is more of a daydream than a reality, yet these folks did it over 200 years ago.

In large part that is why the US Constitution (Version 1.5) has been able to survive as long as it has.

Well-designed software systems behave, very much the same way.

Good software systems are changed only because requirements change. There are few changes for correction of defects. Software systems are sometimes changed to meet new requirements and goals. When changes are needed, the new requirements are prioritized by the stakeholders, usually in a common sense manner. A well-designed software system doesn't require a lot of tinkering once it is built.

Software systems become obsolete for just a few reasons. One is when there are changes to the goals and requirements. Another is when a System is replaced because of changes in technology.

Systems also become obsolete when there is too much volume. Software systems generally have limits on the volume of activity they are expected to support. Even worse the speed at which those volumes increase usually is a lot faster than people expect when they designed the software. At that point, the volume far exceeds the largest estimates for which the software system was originally designed. That is when volume itself can clog the system. Then the system can no longer meet its original goals.

In the software industry, we've learned that once a system is running, the cost of operating the system will in the end be much more expensive than anyone originally anticipated, in part because it will run far longer than anyone expected.

Architects suggest companies should replace a system when there are huge reasons to do so. Sometimes, it is because the time and cost to replace the system is less than the cost of keeping it running. Sometimes it is suggested because the alternative may be to lose the business. Sometimes it is suggested so that the company can stay in business at all. This is when systems are changed in a crisis mode.

Overall, the goal is to continue to make the system meet the initial goals along with the added goals that the organization now has. Those goals can include making a product faster, or better, or in a way that costs less.

Sometimes, the organization says, "never mind" but more often the decision to go forward with a new system happens because the survival of the business depends on making the changes.

As software systems age they become more and more like badly designed systems. It becomes more difficult to manage the software changes. It becomes harder to control the scope of the system (what the system actually does). It becomes difficult to remember what the original goals were which makes controlling the current goals even more difficult. As software systems become outdated, processes and rules become unwieldy. Only the people who "know" the system are allowed to make changes. Sometimes all the reasons for which the system was built become irrelevant as the techs spend most of the time just trying to keep the system running.

There are some government software systems still running today that have reached the point where the original designers have all retired or died. The original developers are long gone. Even the managers and support people are those who inherited the system. In addition, not knowing where the system documentation is wrong is more common that anyone admits. Now, we have the real situation that no one really knows why some pieces of the system were developed in a particular manner. But, even though we can't change them, we still run these software systems because we can't afford not to use them.

Look at the federal government as a system the same way we look at modern software systems. When you do, I think you will agree it has gotten to be like an old software system?

The constitution was designed for a different time. Today's technology would have stunned most of the signers of the constitution just by the speed of the communication. They may have been in shock over the progress made in so many areas of science, the arts, and even politics. It' is likely that one or two of the signers would have decided they had lost their minds if they were transported to today's world. I believe that some of the original designers who would be delighted with the technologies we have today. But I'm also pretty sure that they would be less than pleased with how things currently work in our government.

Right now, our system of government is no longer based on clear priorities. Our system of government is not even based on agreement by those in government on the role that government should have in our lives. In fact, our government doesn't seem to have consensus on anything at all.

As a result, changes to our system cause more and more problems. Each change is not a result of an agreed upon set of priorities. Worse, each change is not based on any agreement at all. Worst of all, changes are not even based on any agreement on how the priorities of our government are even to be considered.

We are now at the point where only "qualified" people participate in that structure. Some of these qualified people are called politicians such as Senators, Congressman, cabinet members and presidents. Others of these "qualified" people are called, technocrats. The technocrats are those who actually run the executive branch operations. Then there are those "qualified" people who try to bend the priorities for good and bad reasons. They are the K Street lobbyists and the special interests and the PACS.

The "qualified" people are those who are able to keep running the current federal government system. They are the current designers and architects of the system. As to how well they work, you may try reading the US Federal Code. Or if you really want to see their handiwork, try understanding the IRS regulations. It has gotten so complex, that the IRS actually tells their help desk personnel to let callers know that they don't guarantee that the answers they give are correct.

You might say that's all well and good, but do we really need a version 2.0 of the Constitution and the Government? For over 225 years the US Constitution has been the glue that has held this country together.

In 1790, most people hoped the Constitution would hold the nation together. Some, like Thomas Jefferson, believed it should and would be rewritten every generation. If you include when the Bill of Rights was sent to the States for ratification it was 225 years old as of September 2014 which is just about 10 generations. (Jefferson may have written some of the most powerful language to form a government, but he was terrible at being a prophet.)

You may think that changing how we deliver the services of the federal government will cause us to lose those services. In fact, "qualified" people in government say that the **"only real"** reason people advocate changing the existing system is to deny people those very services. That type of claim essentially says don't trust anyone. It says the only people you can trust are those who are "qualified" to say what you should be provided and how you should be provided these services. Bluntly put, those people are wrong. And this book is about why and how they are wrong.

This book does not advocate change in order to alter the goals of the service delivery. Rather, this book supports change because it is the only way to improve on what clearly has become an inconsistent, unequal, and therefore unfair delivery system. The one thing that is doubtful is that you believe that the way services are delivered today is the best way possible.

Just because you agree that there can be an improvement in the delivery of federal services also doesn't mean let's chuck the entire system and start over. This book does not suggest starting over at all.

The key strength of the US constitution is that it has mechanisms that work reasonably well to change the system itself. As a country we already have had one occasion in which the system itself did not work. We should be grateful that it only once failed. The last time the system itself failed, those in the North called it the Civil War, while some in the south, even today, call it "The War of Northern Aggression". Will we reach that point again? Let's truly hope not. But, when large segments of the population believe that government can't be fixed, it is close to that last stage of a system, when it can't be changed in a controlled manner at all.

Uncontrolled changes to government systems have a long history. We generally call them revolutions, coups, conquests, or societal collapse. We like to believe it can't happen here in the United States, but we could be wrong. The founders gave us a way to upgrade our systems, so we shouldn't let our fears lock us in place. We will know that it's too late when the US changes government through one of those more common ways.

We do have the ability to use technology to make government work for people, to be run by the people, and be of the people, which is not a bad goal whether it is 1789, or 1861 or today. What's more, there is still time to evolve our government to better serve the entire population, if we keep in mind the benefits of 250 years of experience and the lessons of 250 years of errors and corrections.

But we need to begin. Now!

I hope that this book will begin a real dialog on where we actually do go from here.

CHAPTER 1. WHAT THE BOOK IS ABOUT

This book is about how using we can use technology better. With technology we can improve on the delivery of services. This is true even for the services that the federal government currently provides. And by using technology in a good way, we can better secure our information. Lastly the book also shows how we can use technology to better help our neighborhoods. Technology can help us to use targeted programs to meet our neighborhood needs. This means we can reduce the overlap and gaps in services.

This entire series of books is to help create a sense of neighborhood responsibility for success. To foster a sense of neighborhood responsibility we first need to foster every individual's success. Applying these concepts we can help the population learn how to be more self-reliant. Each person can then pursue his or her unique individual goals. To understand that aspect of the book, you'll need to read a lot more.

SOMETIMES A NEW PERSPECTIVE HELPS

The beauty of the original Constitution is that we can replace the way we do things. And we can do that without having to throw out the whole structure.

During the original Constitutional Convention the delegates from the states were arguing how laws should be created. They had been getting nowhere in deciding how it would work. The delegates also were unable to decide whether the legislature needed one house or two. Lastly, they were unable to agree with each other over how many people were to be in each house, and how they would even be elected into these Houses. As you may imagine, the delegates wanted to make sure that their state didn't get the short end of the deal.

Benjamin Franklin was the oldest person at the convention. He often needed to be carried into the hall where they were meeting. He decided to make a point to the delegates by telling one of his stories. Well, actually, by that time he was so old, he would write out his comments, then have someone else stand up to read them loudly enough for all the delegates to hear. Some people believe Old Ben did that so he could better see how his words affected the delegates.

The story Ben had to tell at first seemed to be just about the Revolutionary War and the Second Continental Congress. Everyone in the room knew the final result of that Congress was the Declaration of Independence. But Ben told them about how that Congress had worked to get people to agree. Clearly the arguments over the Declaration of Independence wasn't really his point.

He talked about a table being built. The goal for the table was to have enough room for the Continental Congress to all sit at the table. He ended the tale with the comments "If a property representation takes place, the small states contend their liberties will be in danger. If an equality of votes takes place, the large states say their money will be in danger. [3] When a broad table is to be made, and the planks do not fit, the artist takes a little from both, in order to make a good joint."

Franklin used the table joining and trimming to make a critical point. It was his way of telling the convention that they needed to spend more time making the parts fit. They needed to stop arguing over who had the best part. By concentrating on how government could work, and how they could actually make the changes, he believed the convention was much more likely to put together changes that were acceptable to everyone.

Franklin's story and this book have that one specific idea in common. This book doesn't go into deep descriptions of why certain pieces of government should be changed. But, at the same time, this book is entirely about what types of changes could and should be made.

------

3 Property in this sense meant the numbers of people who owned property who could become the basis of the electorate, which by the current era, has now evolved to where it would be clearer if he simply spoke in terms of population. In addition, when he speaks to equality of votes, he's simply referring to each state receiving an equal number of votes in the legislature. Today Franklin would have said something like, "If states with more people have larger representation, the small states contend their liberties will be in danger. If equal votes are given to each state, the large states say their rights would be in danger from the smaller states".

The Declaration of Independence and the Bill of Rights describe the core rights and freedoms that we have. These are the rights that the government is expected to protect. Safeguarding and protecting these rights can be seen as requirements. Using that perspective, then ensuring those rights and continuing to protect those rights is one of the core goals of government.

It only makes sense to want to know what effects technology has on our freedoms. The risks our rights have from technology should be obvious. We are seeing them in headlines, in talk shows, in what we buy (such as identity theft protection) hackers, secure networks, password theft, data protection etc. But if we want to protect our rights, we must start to consider what technology can do to protect our rights, not just the threat it raises to our rights.

In so many ways the Information Age presents a new kind of challenge to our rights, but it also presents new tools to protect our rights. These tools fundamentally can change the way we deliver services while improving on the protections that government can provide to our rights.

These tools and changes can change the delivery of services in many ways. It can chance the way we receive services from the US Postal Service. It can change the way we confirm what taxes we owe. It can change the way the VA helps our disabled veterans. It can fundamentally change the footprint of government for the better, if we only accept the challenge.

Some conservative readers will only agree with those changes which make government cost less. Those individuals clearly can see the benefits of such changes.

They may even see benefit in reducing duplication of services as a way to simplify the government. However, if they want to have only the parts that they agree with, as Benjamin Franklin said, the table will never be trimmed and joined.

Some progressives will only agree with the changes that better protect the "civil rights" of people. These progressives will object to using competition to reduce the cost of government almost by reflex. They will rant against any change to make the federal government smaller. They too will need to reach beyond their views. Some of them may even come to recognize the threat to all of our civil rights and recognize the need to compromise on methods even while remaining resolute in the need to protect those rights.

Some people will agree only with the changes that remove the information from government control. They may agree with the changes proposed for the IRS, even to the point of saying the IRS needs to be abolished. They may believe that changing the procedures within a single agency will better protect them. Unfortunately, they will find that they are not protected at all. They may believe that being anonymous is a protection. How well can they be protected when anonymity is impossible?

Some people will agree with the creation of the FNO. They will see if as a way to reduce the concentration of power in Washington DC. These people will reject any changes beyond that point, which will neither protect their rights, nor improve the government, it will simply distribute the disease.

Some libertarians will agree with the changes that protect the rights of the individual from the government more effectively. They can see the threat from what is in place today. However, in doing so, they will opposing any other form of government as an attack on their personal independence. Even when that new form of government actually reduces the weight of the government.

Each of these groups, and the millions of people who don't fit any particular stereotype, need to have their views aired, and considered. They certainly need to have their views represented. Perhaps this book will aid in that discussion just a bit.

The changes this book describes are not meant to impose the will of any group over any other with one exception. The FNO is meant to reflect the valid community interests in the delivery of government services. The FNO is meant to provide a focus on the community's real needs. The FNO is meant to provide a restriction on spending money which is not needed in the community. It is designed to be an alternative to the rampant spending which results in a one size MUST fit everyone. The FNO is intended to do so this in a way that reflects the best of our heritage. The FNO is designed to do so in a way that protects against the worst horrors of our history as well.

Re-architecting government is all about what and how the government should be changed. Since this book is about a re-architected government, then knowing what needs to change is of critical importance. It doesn't really matter what changes a single individual would like government to have or even where government is supposed to go. It does really matter where the American people including you the reader, want government to go. It does matter if you believe that we must change the tools of government in order to both preserve the goals and to meet the requirements of government.

The new terms, concepts and agencies in these books are meant to be a simple way to describe how to change our government to better support our basic rights. In supporting those rights we must be considerate of protecting those rights from abuse by each other. And we must consider how to protect ourselves from abuse by the government. Technology can provide others with new ways of abusing our rights. But those same tools can provide better protections if we use the new tools effectively.

SO WHERE DO WE GO FROM HERE?

Have you ever tried to use a map where all the place names are in a different language? It is hard. Or had a child ask you where you were going, when the reason you are just driving around is to get them to go to sleep. Or the famous question from the back seat "Are we there yet? I'm tired." Or even worse, have your significant other accurately announce that you are lost, and then ask sarcastically "OK so where are we then?" Those three questions can be maddening when you are driving, you're tired, you don't know how much farther to the next rest stop, and your patience is just about as far away as the coffee you drank this morning.

Actually, can any of us actually answer any of these questions about our government today? Probably not. The funniest part is that the kids and spouse never asked how much it would cost to get there, which is a question we often ask about the government.

Using the analogy of the map the answers to those very same questions of managing our government still comes down to "where are we?" , "where are we going? ", and "how do we get there? " . Being able to answer those questions is critical to understanding the path to improving the government and, if needed, the Constitution.

And consider these very real concerns about costs of government.

- If you don't know how much it costs to provide a service currently, you **can't** know how much any change to that service will cost.
- If you don't know the size of a change you **can't** tell how much the change will cost either.
- If you don't know how much what has already been promised to be delivered, you **can't** tell if you can actually pay for it.

If we expect to control how our government works these questions are critical. If we expect to improve how government delivers the services that it provides, the answers are crucial. How often have you heard politicians claim to be able to fix government? How seldom in his backup campaign literature does a candidate talk about the costs, the impacts, and the expenses? You know they haven't evaluated the scope of the change. You know they really haven't thought about the impact of the change. And you know that if they considered the cost of the change at all, they've hidden it, if not outright lied to you about it.

When you think about it, we have promised a lot to ourselves. We've promised public pension plans at both the state and federal government levels. We've made commitments to paying out Social Security benefits even to those who made no contribution. We've hidden the cost of the Affordable Health Care, Medicare and Medicaid. We have special interests getting things by Earmarks, and complex ways through things like Quantitative Easing. The list of these kinds of things goes on and on and on. And even when you are told how much it will cost do you trust the estimate?

Rather than confronting this problem head on, we have today's Washington DC. DC is where the government is based on two parties with power. It's the place where neither party actually welcomes diversity of opinion. We, as the electorate may begin to believe that we have no real voice.

So what are we to do? In over forty years of working with both people and computers, there are a few hard-earned lessons which can be termed laws of imminent system failure, within the computer or the human systems which surround them.

- Law 1 – The surest sign of imminent failure is when the people who maintain of the systems lie to themselves about a problem. This will

inevitably cause the lie to be told to others and
NEVER fixes the problem.
- Law 2 - Fixing the wrong problem is always
  worse than the original problem.
- Law 3 - Replacing an old system is harder than it
  was to build the original system in the first place.

If we think of the federal government as a system,
haven't we all been guilty of allowing Law 1, which is
lying to ourselves about what the problems are, again
and again? Almost certainly, we have.

Law #2 requires some explanation. At its core, when
you fail to fix a defect in the system by the change that
is made, there result two (and probably more) problems
to fix. There is **still** the original problem that wasn't
fixed. In addition, you now have the problem of telling
management that the original problem was not fixed.

Now you may have new problems that the change
caused. First you have the problems because you didn't
think the solution through. Second you have new
problems because you misidentified what the change
would do. Thinking about Law 2 you begin to realize
that politicians have made entire careers out of lying to
us, their bosses and worse never even admitting that a
mistake was made, much less trying to go back and
correct their mistake..

Law #3 says you can replace any system even a
governmental system. But Law #3 says it is a painful
implementation in almost all cases. Even when the
requirements stay the same even if the implementation
is just to upgrade software replacing a system is
difficult. But the most difficult to deliver is when it's

necessary to upgrade and replace an entire delivery system.

Law#3 is included here, just in case anyone thinks replacing systems is easy. It is not.

So where should we go from here? Think of this book as a road map of where we could take this country just a bit at a time. It took 225 years to get to where we are, but we can certainly improve that in less than a generation if we all realize that it's needed to save our future and our children's future.

CHAPTER 2.   HOW THIS BOOK IS ORGANIZED

My son rightly pointed out, "Forget the theory. Just tell them why it's good for them". This book is organized differently than you would expect a "How do we fix the government" book for that very reason. For example, what was initially the first chapter is now just a part of Chapter 15 - Critical Requirements.

Both this book and Volume 2 – Design and Implementation Planning really are a single conceptual unit. Just as in large software systems, understanding the domain, the concepts and the framework should precede the Design. As a result, this book concentrates on first the "what" of the changes which comprise Government 2.0. Then, this book provides a bit of insight into the "why" of the changes proposed for Government 2.0.

Lastly this book focuses on the "who and how" of the changes included in Government 2.0. This is so the reader can better understand and evaluate whether it is worth the rewards of the efforts to make it happen.

The second book has some information about how these changes could happen. That book also contains initial estimates of how much money it will cost, and save. These will not be final figures. Instead they will be what is called a ROM estimate. ROM stands for Relative Order of Magnitude. Finally, book 2 also has some suggestions on how to begin the process to get the public to demand Government 2.0.

CHAPTER STRUCTURE

This book contains the basic pieces of Government 2.0. The "pieces" include the new agencies, some new laws, and a new structure which over time will be added to the government. These "pieces" are what is called design components. These components and how they fit together is what is called the architecture of a system.

The first 14 chapters break this down into more easily understood pieces.

"Chapter 3 – Acronym and Component Summary' contains short definitions of the major components. These components are the core of the changes in government 2.0. These core concepts make government more accessible by each person. And these core concepts are what allows each person to have a greater input to the government.

"Chapter 4 Stories" contains of descriptions of how people can interact with different pieces of Government 2.0. You can think of this as the "How will it work?" explanation in normal English instead of geek speak. In addition to the story itself, features of one or more components are described in slightly more detail. This allows you to begin to get a feel for the shape, size, capabilities and limits on how each component would operate.

Chapters 5 through 8 contains more complete detailed descriptions of the major components that are part of Government 2.0. These components reflect changes needed to more effectively protect the freedoms and rights of the individual.

Chapter Nine titled "Why Architect Government That Way" describes the thinking that lead to Government 2.0. Initially this and the next two chapters were all one huge chapter. It's now been split to make it easier to read. The first part of this chapter is about the external drivers. These are the forces which pushed thinking towards making a change in the way government works. The drivers also made thinking about how to change government in a way to make it easier to both be a part of government, and for government to be a help.

Chapter 10 titled "Aging Federal Systems" describes more about the pieces of government that must be changed to work effectively.

Chapter 11 titled "Component Drivers of the New Architecture" described the new pieces to the entire system. It is through the drivers and frameworks which form Government 2.0 that we can understand the architecture better.

Chapter Twelve titled "New Federal Agencies" describes some new agencies. These agencies are needed to coordinate building the new components and structures. These new structures are first set up in simple form. Then as Government 2.0 grows, these new structures change more and more.

Chapter Thirteen titled "Agency Changes" describes changes made to existing Federal Agencies. These changes are just a sample of the kinds of changes that will happen. As more of Government 2.0 is delivered these changes will become more and more obvious.

Chapter Fourteen is titled "Supporting Components". This chapter contains descriptions of support components added to Government 2.0. Support components help to tie the current pieces of the federal government to the new features of Government 2.0 together.

Chapters 15 through 17 describe the basic requirements which affect Government 2.0. This portion of the book ends in Chapter 17 which contains recommended changes to federal law. These recommendations are to support not only the existing rights of people but also the protections being added into Government 2.0 as requirements. These three chapters link the government of today to what the government must do tomorrow.

Chapter 15 titled "Critical requirements" describes our civil rights as the main requirements for Government 2.0. If we consider our rights to be requirements, we can better understand what government is supposed to do. It also gives us a better idea of what government is not supposed to do.

Chapter 16 titled "Hierarchy of Requirements" contains a way of looking at rights which guided many of the changes. This was especially true from the perspective of what rights are.

This section closes with Chapter 17 titled "Changes to the law" in support of the requirements and the architecture. It describes what the government is required and what government.is not supposed to do.

Chapter 18 titled "Final Thoughts and Coming Attractions" contains conclusions about the vision described in this book. Chapter 16 also has an overview of the contents of the next book in this series. That book is called Volume II "Design and Implementation Planning".

SHOULD EVERYONE READ THE WHOLE BOOK?

It would be great if anyone who reads this book savors each word. But that is not going to happen. At least two thirds of this book is of interest only to readers directly involved in technology, architecture or the federal government.

Other readers may have been drawn to read it because they are liberals. Some may have picked it up because they are conservatives. Still other people may be told to read is because they are libertarians, or any of a dozen other flavors of political viewpoint. Regardless of what view you have, the best suggestion I can make is to read the book according to the perspective that you have. Don't let the talking heads on TV or the news columnists, or those online tell you what the book means. Simply put, make up your own mind about the book.

For those of you who do have a preconceived view, here is a suggested reading sequence. First, you should read the next chapter which gives a relatively short description of each of the new components of Government 2.0. Then read the short essay which most closely matches your perspective, from among the essays in the appendix. You should be able to find a one based on the title that matches your preference (or at least one that you may find funny).

If you are a progressive you should read "Chapter 4
Stories", followed by "Chapter 15 Critical Requirements"
and then "Chapter 18 "Final Thoughts and Coming
Attractions".   Or, if you are a conservative you should
read only those same chapters. I believe you will each
read something of benefit to you. This way you won't
find your blood pressure rising.

For the rest of the book readers, I'd suggest selecting
topics from the chapter headings you would like to
know more about. Of course you could read the entire
book as well.

GOVERNMENT 2.0
THE VISION

CHAPTER 3.   COMPONENT SUMMARY

These components are the focus of the stories in the next chapter, so a brief description of each component is presented here. In most places from here through the end of the book, items are described as though they already exist. That is to make it easier to think about each piece of the new architecture.

FEDERAL NEIGHBORHOOD OFFICE (FNO) -

The Federal Neighborhood Office (FNO) is a new office of the federal government. Each FNO office is small. There are enough FNO offices that most people can actually go to one in their own neighborhood. Each FNO is managed by a locally elected board. That way people can exercise some local control of how the government services are delivered in their community. By using the FNO, people can receive better service from the federal government.

The FNO is a new way for an individual to talk and act with the federal government. What's more, the FNO is a new way for the local community to access federal services. And most importantly, it's a way for the community to have a say in the way services are delivered in their neighborhood.

There are expected to be about 75,000 separate FNO offices. This number is based directly on the number and size of the US Census tracts developed by the US Census Department. That means that each FNO would normally have between 2,000 and 5,000 people in the area supported by the FNO. Normally, a maximum of 7,500 people are expected to be in a single FNO.

FNOs will improve many federal agencies. Today almost all federal agencies have separate offices in the cities. Sometimes the federal offices for one agency are next door to the offices for another agency. The FNO is a single office for people in a neighborhood to access all federal services. Since the FNO is managed by a local board, there will be better community control of the local FNO operations.

The FNO will be the local post office and the local Social Security Administration. The FNO will be the local Civil Rights Commission and the local EPA. The FNO will be the local Veteran's administration and the local federal welfare program offices. Each agency will be changed to use the FNO to deliver services to the people in the community. At the same time the agencies will also be changed to drop the customer operations that have been moved to the FNO.

Each FNO will be serviced by one or more GAAs who report to a locally elected board. A GAA is a Government Authorized Agent and it is described further on in this chapter.

PERSONAL DATA STORE (PDS)

The Personal Data Store is called a PDS. Each PDS is really a special cloud storage account. Each person's

PDS will be made available from a variety of commercial vendors such as HP, Dell, IBM, etc. These commercial vendors could even include small companies operating within the FNO area.

Each PDS is owned by the individual citizen. Each PDS contains as much or as little personal data storage and information as the owner decides. Most vendors will provide a link to personal social networks such as Facebook, if the vendor makes the linkage available, and the PDS owner wishes. The PDS will always have folders for the different kinds of information which the US government needs use in order for the government to perform its services.

Personal Data Store (PDS) accounts are NOT owned nor maintained by the government. Instead the PDS owner decides where he wants his information stored. He does that by selecting to use the PDS storage package of any company which meets the minimum-security standards. These standards are designed to insure that there is a proper balance between security and access. Doing this protects the individual from access by hackers.

Hacking is an access of the PDS which is not authorized. That means government employees who access the information without leaving a record of why they accessed it are hackers as well.

The Security Standards which PDS accounts must meet will be set by the Federal Information Service as a standard. Companies must meet that standard in order to be allowed to be GAAs for PDS accounts.

The Security Standards which PDS accounts must meet will be set by the Federal Information Service. Companies must meet that standard in order to be allowed to be GAAs for PDS accounts.

After the FNOs and the PDSs begin to be built, there will be at least 100 different companies offering their own version of PDS accounts. When finally fully running there will be over 325 million PDS accounts.

For people who refuse to pay for their PDS or who cannot afford to pay for it, a reduced version of the PDS will still be built. If necessary the government will pay for this reduced version.

No matter who actually pays for the PDS it is still the property of the individual.

Individuals at any time may decide to start using their PDS. At that time, they can begin to add their own personal information once they have accessed their PDS. To get into their PDS the first time individuals will need to use a Federal ID Card (FIC) which they can get at any Federal Neighborhood Office. The very first time they access their PDS they will need to be able to scan and read their Federal ID Card. Most of the time this will happen right at the FNO.

GOVERNMENT AUTHORIZED AGENT (GAA)

A Government Authorized Agent (GAA) is a general term for a person or company who is allowed to perform a service as part of the federal government. One type of GAA is a federal employee who is allowed to access a portion of a person's PDS. Another type of GAA is a person who works for a company which provides a service to a government agency or to the FNO. Companies which process tax returns for an individual or family are good examples of GAAs. A PDS vendor is also a GAA. Even the janitorial staff at the FNO is a GAA.

The key is that GAAs are specifically authorized to perform one or more defined processes for the government. And the GAA can be tracked as to what information they view, or use to do that process. This means that any access beyond what they are allowed to do as part of their job can also be tracked. And that access can be logged. And that access can be reported, and if needed, prosecuted.

FEDERAL IDENTIFICATION CARD (FIC)

The US Federal Identification Card (FIC) is a card issued to every person in the US who uses the Federal Government. The FIC card is encrypted. That way, the FIC can be used to identify the person uniquely.

The FIC can also be used by the owner to access their PDS. This includes all the portions of the PDS, such as the Federal Government and Health Insurance Wings. The card can contain personal bank and debit accounts reflecting amounts owned by the individual. This would include amounts from various US Federal Agencies or even personal bank accounts of the individual. It could be used, for example, as a SNAP card (replacement for the Food Stamp Card).

The cards are made by a number of companies who must meet the standards defined by the Federal Information Service. FICs will need to be issued to everyone in the United States even those who are not citizens. In all, about 350 million cards will be issued.

BUSINESS DATA STORE (BDS)

Like the PDS, the Business Data Store is a cloud storage account which has a set of folders which belong to each Business Entity. A Business Entity is a general name used to include businesses, organizations, and associations.

Each BDS contains sets of data that the government needs to be able to access in order to perform its job, but which belongs to the business entity. The BDS cloud storage account is owned by the business NOT owned by the government. Just like the PDS, the Business may use the cloud storage accounts. These accounts just like the PDS must meet the US Federal Information Service Business Data Store Standards.

There will be more than 50 of such private companies providing BDS cloud accounts when the BDS information sets are operational. These companies will support over 18 million BDSs.

In general when this book refers to PDS, the same function applies to the BDS.

In the BDS there are no medical record folders. There won't be any optional folders or wings that would be appropriate only for an individual, such as student study records. But, the BDS wing also will contain some folders which would not normally be needed for a person such as SEC filings.

FEDERAL LOCAL MAGISTRATE COURT (FLMC)

The Federal Local Magistrate Court (FLMC) is an addition to the Federal Courts. Federal misdemeanors are first tried in the FLMC. Most misdemeanors are a part of what today is called administrative law. These are courts and cases which have built up over time as part of the executive branch. The first type of cases to move to the FLMC will be privacy and civil rights cases. The FLMC will focus on these kinds of cases while other kinds of administrative law are redesigned.

The FLMC is expected to operate at the local community level. The FLMC is expected to be only part time. The FLMC may even be virtual in a significant number of cases.

The judges in these courts are actually just magistrates. These magistrates are members of the local community who have had specific training.

FEDERAL INFORMATION SERVICE (FIS)

The US Federal Information Service (FIS) is a new department in the executive branch. The FIS is part of the Government Accountability Office (GAO). The FIS will also have a dotted line relationship to the Office of Management and Budget (OMB)[4].

The FIS is responsible for all the FNO operations procedures. The FIS is also in charge of setting the standards for PDS storage vendors. THE FIS sets the standards for both the service contracts for the FNO and the FLMC and such things as the FIC. Finally, the FIS manages the variety of Programs and projects which are part of Government 2.0.

Other terms (and acronyms) are available as part of the Appendices.

---

[4] While it is critical that the FIS be at a level to command both the support and the input from the other federal agencies, whether it is an additional legislative branch organization, or a part of the executive branch, it could just as easily be part of the OMB and dotted line to the GAO.

CHAPTER 4. STORIES

INTRODUCTION

The chapter contains stories of how parts of Government 2.0 will work. Each story is followed with more information about the component described in the story. I hope the stories accomplish several things.

The stories show how the federal government can do a better job of protecting people's rights. The stories also show how people can have more of a say in their government. These stories all show additional ways our governmental systems should work better. Most important is that the stories show how we can make the systems themselves support the interaction of people with the federal government.

There had been more stories in this chapter but given how many of them were actually written, some of them were moved to the Appendices. If you enjoyed these, you may want to jump into the Appendix and come back before you jump into the architecture.

There are a few important points to remember about the stories.

1. The stories in this chapter and the ones in the appendix are do not completely describe Government 2.0. These stories are just a way of describing how the system can work better. The stories should help you get a better understanding of the capabilities of Government 2.0.

2. The stories and a large portion of this book are written in the present tense. I've found it's easier if you just make the leap into describing what could be as though it already exists.

3. For me to believe that one person could design all the changes that should go into something like re-architecting the government is very arrogant. While I'm confident in my abilities, but I'm not that full of myself. (Although my children may disagree). Everything in this book is simply a way of pointing out how change will happen, either by design or by chance. I believe designing the change is better than having to have things crash and burn before we start to change.

STORY 1. JOHN'S EMAIL – THE EMAIL AND GOVT WINGS OF YOUR PDS

One of the themes of this book is the idea of an electronic home called the PDS. This idea that the PDS is owned and controlled by each individual changes the idea of what we can do with government getting services to us. Control means we can decide who gets access to our information, or at least that we will be told when the government reads our information. Owned means that we get to decide what company will provide the PDS to us, and what other services we want to add to the PDS.

As you will see, the PDS can be used for many different things. But the first practical use for most people is for their mail.

THE STORY - JOHN'S EMAIL

John and Jane Doe are married, and have a house in a suburb of Des Moines, Iowa. Like most people, John has secure access to his computer and to the internet. This morning John uses Google Mail to read his daily mail. He also uses Google as his Personal Data Store (PDS) vendor. He had switched from the Yahoo PDS the year before when Google added more memory into his base plan, in exchange for him tolerating some additional ad space.

When John opens his email he finds the following:

- Three bills which need to be paid,

- a couple of ads that until a couple of years ago, had simply clogged his actual mailbox,

- normal emails with links to the grandkids pictures,

- a notice from Google,

- a notice from H&R Block, and lastly

- A notice from the US government.

The Google notice was that the Government Wing (Government folder in his PDS) had been accessed by the federal government. The notice included a link to a web page inside his PDS. The link lists each government agencies who had accessed his Government data within the last 24 hours, the last month, and the last year.

If he opens the link he would find two notices.

H&R Block as a Government Authorized Agent (GAA) for IRS services had accessed the Government Wing of his PDS. The access noted that H&R Block had done so giving the reason as calculating his annual tax return. The Department of Health and Human Services had opened his information as well. HHS had accessed his information to see if he was eligible for federal money for his health care insurance. This was part of the Affordable Care Act.

Neither of these notices was actually a surprise. Previously John and Jane had decided to use H&R Block for calculating their federal tax return. They had used H&R Block in the past, and since they were now a GAA, the Smiths decided to continue using them. When he had selected H&R Block, he had marked his agreement with them to check his eligibility for federal support for his health care costs which explains the HHS access. More about this portion of John's email story continues later in this chapter.

DESCRIPTION OF THE PERSONAL DATA STORE (PDS)

Most people will think of their PDS as simply a new part of their email. The other benefit to the PDS is that the user can see who in the government is accessing their personal information. The federal government needs access to people's information. Everyone agrees that access to the information is needed for the government to do its job. But it doesn't mean that everyone in the federal government should be able to read your information at any time they choose.

As the PDS gets used more, most people will see more and more benefits. For the sick who can't use email, or for those with religious objections, support services available from the Federal Neighborhood Office (FNO) will help make sure they get their mail.

More information regarding the PDS structure can be found in Chapter 7.

STORY 2. INDIVIDUAL PRIVACY AND THE PERSONAL DATA STORE (PDS)

People have a right to control their own electronic identities. The PDS is designed so that people can control what information is kept there. The design allows the owners to know who accessed their information. This includes when any GAA accesses information within the Government Wing. People have a right to be in control of their own identities, but that right must be balanced. The GAAs help to provide that balance. GAAs provide the way that government can access the information. And the GAA helps to provide that balance by telling the owner about the access.

GEORGE AND HIS RIGHT TO PRIVACY

George has had a few problems with his Social Security Income History. He wants to be sure that the issues get resolved before he retires. The FNO services representative referred George to the Social Security Administration (SSA) who matched him up with a specialist named Steve. The FNO believes that will be the best way to help George with his concerns. George believes his problem was that he wasn't showing any Social Security contributions from 1991 through June of 1994. George outlined his concerns about the missing history to Steve. Steve in turn agreed to look into it. When Steve called George back about the missing data, Steve knew all off George's employment history. This not only included the missing years but everything from 1982 right through the present.

When George looked through his PDS Access Log, he did not see where anyone from the SSA had looked at his information. In fact, the last recorded time they accessed his data was almost 8 months ago. Because Steve seemed to know all about his full employment history, George is now convinced that his data has been hacked. George then contacts IBM (his PDS provider) to see what they know about how his data was accessed.

After hearing George, the IBM service representative agreed there might be an issue. So the rep begins a review of everyone who accessed George's PDS. He even included accesses using George's own ID. At the same time the IBM rep contacted the Federal Advocate at George's FNO. He explained George's concern to the rep. The Federal Advocate reviewed the information and then notified the Federal Information Service (FIS) of the potential breach. If George had initially contacted the FNO advocate, they would have notified IBM as well. No matter who George spoke with first, the FIS, the FNO and the PDS vendor would all have been contacted.

The FIS contacts Steve back at the Social Security administration. It was Steve who was the original source of George's concern. The FIS confirms based on their interview with Steve that his PDS had not been hacked. The information that Steve had obtained which caused George's concern was archived data which had yet to be moved to his PDS.

George is notified that his PDS had not been hacked. In fact no one had meant to violate his rights violated at all. Steve had gotten all of his information from the archived data at the SSA which had not yet been purged. The data hadn't been purged because it hadn't yet been fully loaded to people's PDSs. And since George was the one who originally requested Steve to research the issue, Steve thought he had permission to access the information in the archives without further approval.

Steve is cautioned that he should be clear to the customer that he may be looking through old archives. If he finds what is needed there, it won't show up on the customer's PDS access log. He should tell customers that until the archives are completely deleted, these types of gaps could arise.

DESCRIPTION OF PDS PRIVACY CONTROLS

The Personal Data Store is a simple concept. Every US citizen and resident alien has **a secure PDS. The PDS** is accessed and controlled by each person. And everyone can get their PDS through a private sector vendor of their choice. With secure access and controls everyone's privacy is protected. Simply put, making people's information secure is easier for a private company than the government.

Why? Because if a company doesn't protect a person's privacy the way a person wants, they can change companies. And while there is a lot of temptation to abuse your privacy by both government and private companies, you can change companies a lot easier than you can change government. It is better to set the system itself up, so that a person's privacy is protected.

This kind of change forces big changes to the way the Federal Government works. By having the data stored separately practical controls for accessing that data becomes possible in ways that simply can't be done today.

The PDS Structures are very much different from the way data is stored in government today. As PDSs are used more and more agencies will need to redefine their entire process. As the process changes, data will be moved to the PDS, and eventually the old archives will no longer be necessary.

By designing into the PDS from the start, the requirement to record who accesses the information, everyone's privacy is better protected. It's the same idea as checking out a book from the library. Each time a person's data is accessed (or checked out), a record of the access is created. What's more, it's also stored in the same PDS, just in a different folder. Any vendor who provides PDSs will have to do so, since this would be part of the laws that set up the PDS structure.

With this protection built in, people's data is better protected. And because of this kind of design, it will be easier to find people who "hacked" the data. It will also be easier to prosecute anyone who accesses the data without reason.

With that kind of design, even government employees will need to obey the privacy protections of the individual. This applies to the PDS vendor's employees too.

STORY 3. A CHILD, HIS PDS AND THE LOCAL FNO

JIMMY JONES AND HIS FIRST FEDERAL INFORMATION CARD

Jimmy Jones is a 7 year old who lives in Hampshire Illinois. It is part of the service area called the Whip-Pur Federal Neighborhood Office. The name Whip-Pur is in honor of the high school mascot. Today, Jimmy and his parents are going to Whip-Pur to receive his first Federal ID Card. It will have a special form which tells people he is a juvenile. This doesn't bother him now, but when he gets to be 16 that may change. His parents and he will also start up his PDS and set up which rooms of his PDS he is now allowed to access without his parents signing him in. This will also set which rooms he needs his parents OK to sign into as well. As a minor, his parents have access to all the rooms unless they and Johnny agree he deserves the privacy. This includes his Hampshire Elementary School Room which he now has joint privileges to along with his parents. While Jimmy is somewhat excited about not having to have his parent's permission, he is mostly excited because Dad said he could have a Facebook page in his own personal area.

DESCRIPTION OF THE FNO AND HOW IT SUPPORTS ACCESSING YOUR PDS

One of the first functions that an FNO provides to most people in the community is to set up access to their PDS. This is done at the same time the FNO issues their Federal ID Cards.

After that, the FNO will provide maintenance and support of the user's access of the PDS. They also become the source for replacement of FICs. As the functions of the US Postal Service become more automated, the local FNO will also take the place of current Postal Stations.

The FNO also must sometimes help the person when needed with the PDS vendor. Or serve as a customer service representative with a Federal agency. Sometimes the FNO must have people who can do both.

These kinds of help are especially needed with the young and the very old. This can include help with lost password, replacement Federal ID Cards, or even billing and payment.

In cases such as the death of a member of the family, the local FNO staff can enable access for surviving members of the family, as long as it has pre-approval from the deceased.

When people can no longer maintain their PDS, the FNO can help. The FNO can help the PDS owner with access and use. They can help their family with getting the right documents filled out by the family and physicians to have the local courts turn over guardianship if needed.

DESCRIPTION OF THE FEDERAL IDENTIFICATION CARD (FIC)

The Federal Identification Card (FIC) is a smart ID card. It is designed to identify individuals uniquely. This is to control access to government services. It can also be set up to get used as a credit card. When the FIC card is set up like a credit card, it can be used to credit to the cardholder government funds from a variety of programs. Not only does it make getting money easier for the individual, but also it could be set up to limit the kinds of things the funds can be used to pay. As an example, it could be set up to exclude paying for cigarettes, or alcohol. For more information on the Federal Identification Card please refer to Chapter 14.

STORY 4 – JOHN'S EMAIL..... THE STORY CONTINUES

Many people don't like the Internal Revenue Service. In fact, many people think of the IRS as an enemy. If we change the way the IRS actually works, a different view of the role of the IRS could end up being created. Changing how the IRS works could actually benefit the taxpayer by making it less painful to do your taxes. And changing the way the IRS works could benefit the government by making it less expensive to collect the money the government is owed.

While we need to change the way the IRS works for business, the first area that is likely to be changed is the individual taxpayer process. Changes for business will happen later, but will work in much the same way especially for small businesses.

As you recall, John had received an email from H&R Block. This story continues with that piece of the government changes for the IRS.

JOHN'S EMAIL FROM H&R BLOCK

The second notice was even more interesting. It was a notice from H&R Block. They had calculated taxes that John and Jane Doe's owed for last year. This was based on everything that had been recorded with the IRS from their employer and their banks. H&R Block calculated their taxes for last year at $34,500 with resulted in a net refund of $600. The calculations were actually shown in the email. This was possible, since their email was secure.

John could simply select a link for John to approve the calculation if he chose. If he did so, H&R Block would complete filing his taxes. At which point his taxes were done. No worry about audits, or the IRS coming back for something that was missed.

John could also select a second link. This link sends John to an H&R Block web site where John could update, correct, or augment the information H&R block had used to complete his 1040.

John selects the link to update the information, John is presented with what is effectively a completed 1040, which he then reviews and sees that there is no record of any charitable contributions. John has donated a lot of money to his church, so he knows that he is missing some deductions that he can and should claim. John then accesses his banking information which he maintains in his Google cloud. Looking there, he identified that he had contributed $2560 to his local church in the past year. Selecting those checks, he creates a list which he uses when he returns to the suggested 1040 screen. There he updates the charitable contributions to indicate the $2560 and the name of the Church that should have a record of his contributions on file, along with pasting the list of checks to the return. The screen recalculates the amount which comes back with a new estimated tax of $32,600 and a net refund of $1275. John then hits Submit on the form, and goes on about his day.

Four days later, he gets another email from Google that his personal information had again been accessed by H&R Block on behalf of the IRS. When he opens it, he sees that it was an access to confirm the updated 1040 he had submitted previously. Just as he closes the email, a new mail shows up from the H&R Block.

Opening that link he sees essentially the same item as he saw the first time which was an accept option which showed him owing gross taxes of $33,600 (which was the value of the updated return he had sent back). He hits accept, and the notification that his taxes had been accepted by John and Jane was returned to the IRS and his taxes for the year were finished.

John knows he can only be audited on his contributions to his church, because H&R Block was responsible for the rest of his return.

Three days later, he receives a notice from his bank that a refund from the Department of the Treasury had been deposited in his bank account.

DESCRIPTION OF IRS CHANGES FOR THE INDIVIDUAL

The changes envisioned for the IRS are substantial. In order to see the full size of the changes, you need to go back to where the IRS began. The ability to charge an income tax was actually the 16th amendment. This gave the ability for congress to levy an income tax. From 1912 until today, this simple idea has become so complex that not only is an entire industry built around it, but also an entire court was created. Why has it become so complex? There are many reasons, but the single biggest reason is that Congress decided to create exceptions to the basic idea of a tax.

This book isn't meant to change the things that the IRS taxes, or even to change the exceptions that Congress has applied over the years. I am not saying what Congress did was correct either. Just that this book is directed towards doing what the executive branch is directed to do by Congress efficiently and effectively.

The problem is that the IRS rules have gotten too complex. Now, not even the Congress or the IRS can provide a clear description of what is to be taxed, and how the taxes are to be calculated.

When the current tax collection system was formed, there was a large portion of the entire revenue system that existed only on paper. You may not remember, but once upon a time, the banks used to use little books as saving account notebooks. These were called passbook savings.

By 1976 when the IRA system started, a huge change was underway for banks. A lot of new information had to be captured by the bank so it could be sent to the IRS. The banks had to report how much they paid in interest. They also had to report how much they collected in interest. Why? So that the IRS could check the paper calculations that everyone did by hand.

In 1975 a lot of income reporting was only a paper trail, there was no electronic trail. Today, the idea of having a paper trail ONLY makes no sense. It also doesn't make sense to have the IRS validate that paper trail, which now only exists so the IRS CAN validate it.

What makes a whole lot more sense, is that everyone report what he or she earn. H&R Block, Intuit, and all the other tax companies sell services which do the same job that the IRS does. That is, they figure out what you owe. Rather than pay to have the same thing done twice, it makes more sense to have the tax calculation companies, submit their process to the IRS to check the PROCESS. Once the process is validated the vendor should be good to go. Everyone who uses that vendor to validate what they owe (or get as a refund) ought to be finished with their taxes.

This changes the way the IRS needs to be viewed. You no longer need to think that the IRS is out to "get" you, or that the IRS has become the enforcement arm of what some see as government mafia. This view actually affects the very ways people even want to interact with the government. If the IRS meant what its name says, that is, a revenue SERVICE, then the attitude of the IRS to the taxpayer will eventually result in the taxpayer changing their view. The basic function of the IRS after all is to collect the *appropriate lawful* amount of money based on the income of the person.

It should not have the primary purpose to pursue the individual or because of confusing, inconsistent and frankly antagonistic procedures cause an annual ethical challenge for both taxpayers and tax collectors alike.

For all the individual taxpayers, the validation of the amount owed will become the direct responsibility of IRS Individual GAA vendors, such as TurboTax, H&R Block and others who have applied for and received GAA status. These vendors in effect act, as agents of the individual who are now responsible for insuring that the individual complies with appropriate tax law. Any audit or review of process information about the tax return will be an audit or review of the GAA not the individual taxpayer.

Further details can be found in Chapter 13.

STORY 5. THE VETERAN AND HIS MEDICAL RECORD

One of the good ideas in the Affordable Care Act is the push to have an electronic Medical Record. Unfortunately, like many other good ideas in the federal government, it went badly wrong. It's not enough to have the record be made electronic. The records are still housed separately. There are separate records for the doctors. Each hospital has their own records. Nursing homes maintain their own information. Even worse is in the government run hospitals, where different VA hospitals each have their own records which aren't shared, or used for the best care for the veterans.

The following story gives both an example of today, and what could be done better tomorrow.

It is unfortunate is that the following story is based on a real life version in today's world. One veteran, let's call him Phil, related this to my nephew.

My nephew who is a veteran, in turn published it as part of his blog. [5] The story itself is from that blog

PHIL'S NOT SO EXCELLENT SERVICE AT THE VETERANS' ADMINISTATION

This is the current VA. Phil had his disability case VA pending for over 17 months at the VA.

"They are trying to decide just what his disabilities are, what percentage, what kind of treatments are needed, etc., etc. I am sure you can fill in the rest, but that isn't what this post is about. But I will add one more point before the meat of this. My friend went above and beyond, and sent in over 100 pages of documentation prior to the VA asking for the documentation.

This post is about Customer Service. Wait…Lack of customer service.

Now, as a veteran, I don't want to be treated better or worse than anyone else in this country. I don't want to be treated special, but I would at least like a modicum of respect, which we should give to every citizen.

So back to my friend, and his head butting with the VA.

---

[5] http://twoperturbedveterans.wordpress.com/2014/09/04/the-va-customer-service-is-a-joke-a-2-hour-wait-to-get-told-to-call-someone-else/

His first call was to his VSO (Veteran Service Officer or the proxy representative for the veteran) who said that his paperwork had stalled due to a medical opinion needed from the in house physician from the comp/pen department.

His next call was to the hospital patient advocate to see if they could find out where the documentation was stalled out and get it moving again. He was told by the advocate that his medical records were with regional and suggested to call the regional number to request information on them.

He called into their regional help line to see why his case has not had any action in the last month (you can look that much up on their website) the next morning because he felt it was not going to be a fast call.

Let's start with the fact that the phone system said to expect a 25-minute wait. The wait was 1 hour and 56 minutes before a human came on the line.

The person who came on the line said, "Your case hasn't moved in a month."

Ok, no kidding. The website said that. The VSO said that. The patient advocate said that yes it had not moved, but since they had time requirements to meet, the information he received was incorrect somehow.

The only other thing that the person who came on the line after two hours said was to call this other person.

This other person is a patient advocate. The patient advocate said, "I have no idea and I will send an email to the Department Head. When asked the name of that person for accountability, the answer was I cannot give out that information....Please call back tomorrow to see if there is a reply to my email."

So, 25% of a workday spent on hold, to be told call back tomorrow?

But let us take a look at the time involved on this one.

- A 17 month wait time for the whole claim from start to now.
- Approximately 2 hours of phone time the day before making various calls to VSO's, patient advocates, voice mails, phone tree's etc.
- 2 hours 9 minutes today on either hold or getting told to call the local hospital patient advocate.
- 10 minutes on the phone with the patient advocate that in the end finished with "call back tomorrow."
- All of this has taken place (the whole process is STILL not over yet) for a process which the VA claims should only take a TOTAL of 120 days.

Now THAT is what I call customer service. ""

By the way, the VA advertises that this entire process should take less than 120 days, while his was now over 500 days with no end in sight.

We can not only do better, we must. In Government 2.0 using the individual's PDS to include their medical records is an obvious outcome and benefit of creating a singular repository of the individuals' information. This would have resulted in ZERO TIME trying to find his record. The problems at the VA in 2014 won't get fixed by a PDS; they go far deeper than that. But at least it's a start. The transition to support this will obviously not take place in a day or even a year, but the benefit to doing so will last a lifetime.

DESCRIPTION OF THE INDIVIDUAL'S MEDICAL RECORD

Part of the individuals Personal Data Store (PDS) is an area for medical records. The Medical Record wing will be able to be accessed only when the owner of the PDS authorizes a health care provider, and then only for the period of time that the PDS owner specifies. This would include personnel at the Veteran's administration.

Refer to Chapter 11 for more information regarding the PDS.

STORY 6 THE INDIVIDUAL AND THE FNO VOTING SYSTEM

SAM AND STARTING THE CHINATOWN EAST FNO OPERATIONS

Sam is a resident of New York City. He lives right down the street from the Chinatown East FNO which just opened. During the 3-month startup period, Sam in addition to registering and receiving his FIC card now has the ability to vote on multiple decisions. These decisions regard those which need to be made in starting up the Center. Sam may vote on the name for the FNO. More importantly, he can vote on the preferred hours of operation. He can also vote for the first elected members of the local management team called the FNO management board. These people will serve until the next scheduled election. Sam can also vote on other things including answering other questions brought by the residents of the FNO.

Once Sam has actually voted on the questions, he has the ability to "lock" in his vote or simply leave it so he can think about it and perhaps change later. If he doesn't return to lock his vote, it will automatically be locked at the end of the voting period.

Sam also can add questions for the next election.

DESCRIPTION OF THE FEDERAL NEIGHBORHOOD VOTING SYSTEM

Federal services in Gov 2.0 are often provided by the FNOS. Most of the time, these services are both provided and managed by the people in the local area. This is the biggest change in Government 2.0. The control begins literally from the time that the local FNO is fully set up. The people who live in the neighborhood which comprises the FNO have the right to vote on who is on the board of the FNO. That allows them to control some of the ways the FNO delivers services to the area. To do that, each FNO comes with election software which will not only is easy to set up but the software itself handles, recording and reporting on election results within the FNO. Because it's electronic, the concept of early voting becomes purely arbitrary. That means, once the ballot questions are set, balloting can start and continue right up to the point where the "polls" closes.

Once the election is finished, the records of who voted for what are dropped from the individual's PDS, and the only remaining record is that the person actually did, or didn't vote.

Refer to Chapter 6 for more info about the FNOs.

STORY 7 THE INDIVIDUAL AND PROTECTING HIS RIGHTS

Civil rights cases are today's major way to fight discrimination. But in the beginning of those cases, it was very hard to prove a case. Now, it is a large process to handle a civil rights case, because not only is a person charged with discrimination, but also companies and groups. It's likely that the companies and groups are the reason these cases are as big as they have become. Part of the reason for this, is that it is the companies and groups which usually have the money to pay for the fine. There is even a term for it. It's called "deep pockets". Some of these organizations are actually at fault more than the individual, but most are not. The "deep pockets" are needed because the cases can be long drawn out and expensive. They are long and drawn out and expensive because there are "deep pockets".

In Gov 2.0, a new kind of court is added. It is called the Federal Local Magistrate Court (FLMC). The FLMC is as different as possible from the locales and settings that civil rights cases are handled today. As an example, the FLMC is run by a part time (hourly) judge, where parties do not require the use of attorneys.

The scope of the jurisdiction of the Federal Local Magistrate Court is in only limited areas, both of which have essentially been transferred from the executive branch as administrative law and federal civil rights violations. The scope of the FLMC is effectively the administrative and civil law which is not already covered by state law within the state that has the specific FNO.

THE STORY – JERRY SMALLWOOD, HIS NEW APARTMENT AND HIS NEW JOB (CONTINUED)

In the preface you read a bit about Jerry Smallwood. He was the new college graduate who was moving to a new town. He needed an apartment. Not only that but he found out how the FLMC can help defend his rights better than today. Now let's continue the story from George's perspective. George was the person who refused to rent to Jerry.

From George's perspective he feels like he wasn't supported by his employer. And because he was actually found guilty and had to pay the fine he thought he wasn't being treated fairly. George contacts an attorney to complain that he didn't have fair representation. The attorney told him that with the changes in the law, he could have requested not only an attorney, but he could have requested that the entire proceeding be moved to the Federal Circuit Court. One serious concern however, was that George would have had to pay the added costs if he lost the case. George said the Federal Advocate had said the same thing, but since that was going to be expensive, he decided to represent himself.

The attorney also told him while he could appeal it was probably a lost cause. With the deposition from Sally at the apartment complex, it would be very difficult for George to win, and he should consider himself lucky to have his job. Although George would like nothing better that to take on this completely new way of looking at things, he thinks he would be better off if he went and found another job.

DESCRIPTION OF THE FEDERAL LOCAL MAGISTRATE COURT

Each FNO will essentially have one magistrate elected by the FNO residents who will serve on the FLMC. The areas covered by several adjacent FNOs will be combined into a single FLMC area, run by a Chief Magistrate. The elected Magistrates will choose the Chief Magistrate for the FLMC. There are expected to be 7 FNOs within each FLMC area. This would result in about 10 to 15,000 separate FLMCs. That's part of the reason why this can be handled by a part time judge.

For more information on the FLMC please refer to Chapter 8.

STORY 8 GOVERNMENT CONTRACTING CHANGES FOR THE FEDERAL NEIGHBORHOOD OFFICES

One change with the FNO is who actually is delivering the service. Today, people are used to working with government employees when they contact an agency. Gov 2.0 changes the way the services are delivered. First, people at the local level will actually deliver the service. That is because the processes are really standardized. Everyone should receive the same level of service. If this is still unclear, think of MacDonald's actually managing the FNO. FNOs will be like a government franchise operation, where small companies can actually get the contract to provide the customer service at an FNO.

Gov 2.0 makes the FNO become the place to receive most government services. People won't have to call the Social Security Administration for one kind of problem. Then when they find out it's another agency, they won't be forced to start all over.

To do this requires a lot of preparation work. But once done, the procedures are all written out. Now, small companies can bid to be the vendor who provides the people at the FNO, who serves the community.

In turn, that means different contracts for each FNO. That's why each FNO runs the same, because they all have the same contract. It's the people providing the service who work for different companies.

When the contract is close to being finished (in government terms that's called expired), the government can either extend the contract or go to another vendor.

 Here's an example which also shows one of the reasons for the FNO board.

RENEWAL OF THE CUSTOMER SERVICE OPERATION AT THE SAUGATUCK CT. FNO

The Saugatuck FNO has a contract with SAGA to provide the customer service at the local FNO. The contract will expire in 3 months. As a result, the FNO Board starts the process to figure out if they are going to change vendors. The FNO Board uses the recommended process published by the Federal Information Service in the FNO Board Operations Manual.

The first step of the recommended process is to post a request for feedback to the residents of the FNO area. The request is asking people whether they are happy with the service. The people have 4 weeks to respond. If they haven't done so within the first two weeks, the local board operating software sends reminders.

At the next board meeting, the results from residents have been received. The first thing noted is that almost 60 % actually responded to the request. The responses showed that over 70% of the community were either happy or very happy with the level of customer service they received from SGA. Only 15% said the service was marginal or poor. The amazing part of those numbers is that this survey got over 60% responding.

Using those numbers, the board looked at the current prices available from all the approved FNO vendors. SAGA's service is 15 cents higher per local resident per month than the next lower priced vendor (Zenith Customer Service) is. The board also can see how other FNOs rated Zenith and SAGA. It was there that the board saw that SAGA rated better than Zenith. Since the number of people in the FNO area is 4,800 the price is only $720 higher for Saga than Zenith per month (well within the discretionary expenditure budget for the FNO).

The Board is happy with the service and the costs that SAGA has been charging. And because the costs between the two vendors is close, the local board decides to continue using SAGA. The Board completes the appropriate confirmation to extend the SAGE contract for the next 3 years, and sends that back to Washington to the FIS.

Had the Board decided not to continue with SAGA, the process to change vendors is also documented. They simply consult the manual from the FIS and switch over to Zenith at the end of the contract.

The other positive to continuing with SAGA is that Frank Reynolds will be able to continue with his responsibilities as the fifth board member as well. That's because Frank was the GAA vendor representative, and with continuing the contract there is no need to change.

DESCRIPTION OF FNO VENDORS

FNOs operate closer to a franchise model than the traditional government model. Companies can be certified to provide these services to one or more FNOs. Contracts are awarded on a competitive basis by each FNO board. These vendors are simply a GAA at the local level.

The board of the local FNO are the only public officials actually paid by the government directly. Even they are paid on the part time basis that is the same as some local government boards are set up today. In the franchise model, they would own one franchise however, like all other public officials the FNO board would be elected.

CHANGES TO FEDERAL AGENCIES DIRECTLY SERVING THE PUBLIC

In Gov 2.0 the federal agencies that serve the public directly have major changes. First, the customer facing side is removed from the agency. That is handled by the FNO at the local level. To make sure that the process is correct, the agency is directly responsible for insuring that the procedures are complete. Once that validation is completed, vendors can describe their capability to provide that service and become a GAA.

For most FNOs, the first GAA is selected before the FNO is opened. That is why GAA contract will initially be with the FIS. After the FNO is opened, the FIS will transfer the contracts to be handled by the FNO board. The board can then on a regular basis renew the contracted GAA or replace the GAA with another approved agent.

This results in a better combination of price and effectiveness than what individuals receive today through the existing agency functions.

DESCRIPTION OF THE FNO BOARD

The FNO Board is a board elected by the voting age residents of the FNO. The board is composed of 5 people. The first four members are directly elected by the residents, and the fifth member is a representative of the local FNO vendors. This fifth member can only vote in the event of a tie. The vendor representative functions essentially as the FNO superintendent to the local board.

For further information about contracting changes refer to Chapter 12.

For further information about the FNO Board, please refer to Chapter 6.

STORY 9 GOVERNMENT GRANT DISTRIBUTIONS THROUGH THE FEDERAL NEIGHBORHOOD OFFICES

There are many other changes to the way government can deliver services in Gov 2.0. One of these changes is how grants can be approved at the local level. Another change is how programs can be managed at the local level. Today, federal grants require their own oversight structure. This means new resources at the federal level. These resources control who gets the grant. The resources control how the grant is managed. In effect, the agency on a national level decides how the grant is used. Sometimes, the agency even needs auditors to check the agency itself. And then there are agencies which just audit other agencies. This takes many people, to find problems that really are the result of bad design.

Government 2.0 can begin to fix this by moving the grant approval to the FNO in some cases. That improves the process and optimizes the grants. It also helps to decentralize the power that the agencies now have. Best of all, it can do so with a level of discretion and management which cannot be done at the federal scale.

Here is just one example for an improvement to the local educational system.

GRANDPARENT TUTORING GRANT AT JEB STUART ELEMENTARY SCHOOL USING FNO AUTHORIZED FUNDS.

Sally Winters is the principal at Jeb Stuart Elementary School. This is the school for the kids in the near North Side in Richmond, VA. The Service area for the school actually includes 3 different Federal Neighborhood Offices. Like all FNOs, the ones each one in the area has a fund for local improvements. Ms. Winters applies to all three FNOs to fund a program for a grandparent-tutoring program managed by the school PTO. The PTO provides the volunteers, the oversight, and the prizes for children who participate in the volunteer program. While the proposal is called the Grandparent tutoring program, it is actually open to all members of the community. All someone has to do is to be both willing and able to tutor students in first through third grade. In turn, the students in need of tutoring are identified and matched to the volunteers. The proposal is for funds to make the program work. That includes funds to keep the building open after school. In her proposal, she identified funds to keep the building secure while it is open. She also included funds to do background checks on the tutors. Lastly, she included a budget for prizes. The proposal had the amount being requested from each FNO, and the total needed to make the program work. The only commitment that the grant proposal makes about the success criteria, is that funds will be used for the purposes described in the proposal, and that the student performance will be measured both before and after each semester they participate in the program. The grant is requested for the full school year by the school.

FEDERAL FUNDING FOR FNO INITIATIVES

The Federal Funding for FNO Initiatives is legislation passed in the 2018 Congress. The law allocated to each FNO a fund they could use for local reasons. These local initiatives had to use standard accounting, but the real focus was to deliver needed services at the local level. Some of these funds were not available at all before the law was passed. And some other kinds of grants were available only if they were managed, and directed by staff in DC.

Ms. Winters under the new law is able to make the application to both the local school board, and the local FNOs at the same time. The local school board application approves the program at their next meeting. They approved the use of the building and to provide some of the support resources needed. These were for the janitorial and security staff.

The FNO board decision to approve or not approve the grant will be based on the local needs. Ms. Winter's proposal seems to apply to an obvious community need. The local board decides that this proposal is one of the more important community needs. That's why they approved it so quickly. The board understands that the funds they can spend locally are limited, but decided it was too important to ignore. It is not expected that federal funds will cover all possible grants which may be requested, and part of the basic responsibility of the FNO board is to prioritize requests for the maximum local benefit.

Because local reading scores have been so much lower than the national average, the three FNO boards determine that they will fund the request for the next year, after which performance characteristics of the students will be used to determine whether the program funds should be made available for the following year. Rather than provide the funds directly to the school, or directly to the school district, the funds will actually be approved to be spent by the FNO board, and then the individuals and business who provide the services identified by the grants will have the funds deposited to the FIC cards of the businesses after Ms. Winters confirms they have actually provided the goods and services, or as in the need for prizes to be obtained to Ms. Winters through a grant specific Federal ID Card credit account just for that purpose.

Further stories can be found beginning in Appendix A.

GOVERNMENT 2.0
THE ARCHITECTURE

CHAPTER 5. INTRODUCTION TO THE ARCHITECTURE

Stories like those in Chapter 4 can give a feel for how a system will work with people. But they really don't define how all the pieces go together. And even more, it doesn't tell you how the system will work. It's the architecture that really described how a system works. That's especially true if you include both people and the software. There is a piece of bad news about architecture. It's really boring. And yet, it is absolutely needed. You see, if you miss pieces in the architecture, you can find that the systems don't actually run very well.

For example, think of the different pieces that go into a bicycle. If you had a complete description of the wheels, and the frame, and the pedals, and the gears you still wouldn't have something you could use very well until you had the description of the handlebars. Without them, you can't control the direction. Even with them, without the pedals, it would only work well going downhill. It's only when you have all the pieces that you can begin to see how a bicycle can get you from one place to another more effectively than walking.

Architects like to use fancy terms for different parts of a system. Sometimes, those terms really do make a difference, but many times, it only makes a difference to another architect. The different pieces which comprise a system sometimes are called subsystems. Other architects use terms like components, which is how it's described in this book. Still other architects use terms like subject areas, or objects, of classes. Regardless of the different names that geeks tend to use, just think of a component as one of the big pieces of the bicycle.

When a system is changed and expanded, sometimes new components are needed. But if an existing component works fine, architects just take the old component and continue to use it. Sometimes, components can work with modification. Then the architect describes the change that is needed for the component. Then developers push the change into the old component. But sometimes, a new component is needed. New components are used when a system has to do new functions, or technology makes better ways of having the component work.

Again, think of the gears on a bicycle wheel. Initially bicycles had only one gear on the back wheel and one gear on the pedal. Many bicycles today still only have one gear. But then 3 speed, 5 speed and even 20 speed bikes were designed. This included modifying existing components, like the added gears on the pedal and the back wheel, or sometimes adding minor components, like the derailleur, (that's the gizmo that helps with the gear shifting so the gears don't lock). But if you want to go a lot faster, you changed technologies, like adding a motor which was so different it gives you something new called a motorcycle.

Even so, without roads, bikes and motorcycles don't work well. So even if you have everything to define the motorcycle, you still need to know the environment where you are actually going to run the motorbike. Are the roads dirt, or cobblestone or modern highways? Each of those variables affect the kind of tires you want on the wheels, but they may not have any affect at all on the handlebars.

The same is true if the system we are talking about is the government system. If we don't need to change a particular piece of the government, we really don't need to spend time and effort describing it. You wouldn't need to describe how the Congress works except for the changes it needs to have. But accurately describing the changes, along with the new items is critical.

At some point as the architects detail the new things and the changes to things you actually move into the design phase. Or at least that is what the techies call it. Design is the point at which the process moves beyond just a description, and begin to describe how the "guts" of a component works. Design also makes sure that everything that is needed for the actual implementation is known and can be available, like the chain grease for the bike.

The difference between the architectural analysis and the design phase is not nearly as clear as techies make it sound. Generally, you have a pretty good idea how one part will work, then you work on another part. But you don't have to have everything in detail down to the last feature like the width of the wheels.

As an example, say you are working on the motor of the motor bike. When you work on the motor, you really don't pay much attention to how wide the wheels are. You pay attention to how wide the wheels are when you work on the axles, or the rims. In architecting changes to a system you always make the assumption, that you know as much as you need to about the pieces of the system you are not changing, even while you are reviewing and defining how new pieces will work.

We assume that we have all the pieces that we need. We can only check this assumption by trying the ideas out. But we do need to remember, that it is a huge assumption, that we have it all. But without that assumption you can fall into a major trap in systems design. It's called analysis paralysis. It is the cause of a lot of programs and projects to failing. You see, when you spend so much time looking over what else could be involved, getting every detail nailed down to the point where everything has to be rechecked every time, you will find out that something has changes and you need to start all over again. I'll leave it to others whether this book has missed something.

The following chapters get into all of that but they begin with the "new" stuff, because every technologist always wants to hear and to present the "new" stuff before it gets too boring, if it hasn't already.

Please remember that at least for the next few chapters, no attempt has been made to identify current components which don't need to change. Also please remember the other "standard keep in minds" of

- This is draft

- This is only to get people thinking about controlled change

- The changes need to be improved

- People need to understand

- And it needs to be validated by testing

- It is written in the present tense only to make it easier to understand

PUBLIC ARCHITECTING - ARE YOU INSANE?

So it should be easy to describe the architecture and then everyone can move forward. If that were true, these changes would have already happened. These changes are neither easy, not simple. But a design for a re-engineered government like this design (or something like it) is needed.

The changes proposed in this book cannot be made in secret. So if for no other reason that necessity, this book assumes it can be done in public. That is the biggest assumption of all with this book.

The second major assumption is that you can plan significant change in government at all. Significant changes, are almost impossible without the threat of force. The usual way that major change happens is by the use of force. Examples of "almost" peaceful revolutions like South Africa, Argentina, Chile all have some form of violence, usually both before and after the actual revolution.

Let's for a moment look back at the Constitutional Convention. First, it wasn't called that. It had various names, including Grand Convention. It actually wasn't the first convention called to fix the Articles of

Confederation. A preceding convention the "Annapolis Convention" had not even had all the states attending. The only useful product of that convention was a call for another convention. Again, does this sound like today?

In Virginia, there was a significant debate in the House of Delegates. Some heroes of the revolution like Patrick Henry refused to attend. Virginia's House of Delegates passed two resolutions. The first was to call on other states to attend a convention in Philadelphia. The second was to elect delegates to the convention including Washington, Madison, and George Mason the author of Virginia's Bill of Rights.

A few other states elected delegates. It would have died there, except that the Confederation Congress (which was the current national government), decided to effectively endorse it by calling for the convention to begin in May. But interestingly, the Confederation Congress agreed only to have a group to propose changes to the current articles.

The members of the convention knew what was starting to happen in France. Many in the states had fears of the British returning, or one state attacking another. When Massachusetts and New York tried to close their harbors to make the British and French pay taxes, Connecticut opened its harbors. What had been won in war, could well be lost in war. But the most basic fear was that the people within each state would rebel against the state and the federal government. Shays rebellion had already happened, and the rebels had even tried to capture a federal armory in Springfield MA. To people in the other states, the start of the original revolution was in Massachusetts. Was another revolution beginning there? Frankly, this scared the members of the convention.

As a result of these worries, the members of the convention knew that something had to be done. Unfortunately no one knew exactly what should be done, or even what kind of change was needed. Options and structures of government needed to be discussed. Delegates needed to compromise. They needed to hear the reasoning behind each idea.

The delegates believed that if you had even discussed any ideas in public, than all the delegates would be forced to take positions. These would be positions they couldn't change. They thought by keeping it secret, each delegate could change his position as the whole group debated.

Doesn't that sound like congress today? With the internet, public statements from decades ago are used to destroy or damage opponents. As a result, publicly changing positions by our career politicians becomes suicidal.

With all of our history showing how effective it was to actually construct the changes in secret, why is this book about doing it all in public? Because there is no other option if you want to have a peaceful orderly change. Either the changes must be discussed publicly, or there can be no change inside the law.

This book assumed that secrecy is NOT needed to design changes in government. That is good because there is not an alternative. There must be a willingness to publicly analyze and publicly design the concepts to improve the government. Those changes must then be sold to larger and larger communities within the country.

Why must the entire process be public? Technology has changed everything. The speed, depth, and availability of information has changed everything.

Technology has changed the way we must consider change. Believing you could change the government today in secret is almost laughable. But that does not mean change is impossible. When the country was founded the information age wasn't even the subject of science fiction. There was no science fiction back then. Even the modern novel was less was less than a hundred years old. Jules Verne was almost a century in the future. The first general purpose computer was over 150 years before it was available.

Instead, think about how quickly information moves today. As a result, the way we change systems also has had to change.

Today we develop changes in software systems through a process which even though it doesn't always work, is better than not using it. Like everything else in information technology it has a fancy term. It is called the Systems Development Life Cycle (SDLC). Using SDLC most system design is done publicly within the enterprise itself. That's because designing anything complex, you need to document how the new functions go together. That's so more than one person can work on it as well as to allow others to check to be sure it will work when you actually build the system.

But before we even get to the design stage of the SDLC, someone has to "see" how the system will go together. That starting point for an architect is what is called the vision. The vision is a shorthand way to describe what functions the system is supposed to support. Architects need that so they can define in some way how the new and old parts of the larger system go about fulfilling those needs. This vision then is "sold" to the designers. The designers then begin to put assumptions together with features that the software system needs to have as a piece of the initial design documents. These documents are so that it is NOT a secret on how the system goes together.

It doesn't matter if a system automated or manual. Architects and the decision makers and owners of the system should understand large changes in detail. You might think that the only people who need to understand the changes before they begin to be implemented is the business owners who must literally buy the change. That's not exactly true. Yes the business owners must first "buy" the concept. Then the owner must sponsor the approach and then fund the development. Finally, the owners must champion or at least approve the implementation. It is only when a system is ready that you really need to have the users buy in. If you want a system to be successful, the people who have to buy it are the people who will actually use the system.

This is perhaps the most significant difference between designing changes into a software system and even attempting to design a change into our system of government.

In government, in theory, people need to not only understand, but approve the change before it starts. The people can then change their mind as opponents make valid (and invalid) critiques of the changes. If that were the standard in software development, no structural changes could possibly occur.

In a perfect world everyone involved in the system should feel comfortable they both understand the changes, and the way that the changes will be incorporated within the system. Obviously, this is not a perfect world. Can you imagine a help desk clerk having to buy into a merger between IBM and Apple? No one expects that to be the situation. Or do we?

Isaac Asimov once observed "Anti-intellectualism has been a constant thread winding its way through our political and cultural life, nurtured by the false notion that democracy means that *'my ignorance is just as good as your knowledge."* Was he right? Is it that we allow screams of ignorance and denial to outweigh every other opinion? It is possible that we have become victims of opinion where facts aren't needed, just a podium?

This book makes the contrary assumption. This book explicitly assumes that by effectively describing a better way, that not only is positive change still possible, but the better way will win the debate. And that really is the heart of the second assumption, that we can change our form of government even while publicly debating, offering alternatives and improvements. Otherwise, while this book may have been written, it most certainly will not cause a change.

It is easy just to write stories, be they short or epics, about how the new governmental systems would function. But the reality is that there does need to be coherence in the design. There must be sense to the integration of components between the new and the existing system for there to be any possibility of change. The changes to the existing systems need to be understood, so that the system changes that need to be made can be successful. This is most critical when the system changes are major.

It is paramount when you are speaking of changes that can affect everyone's future.

So think of the next chapter about the Federal Neighborhood Office as the first jagged draft of that SDLC. It is the first of the components that need to be described. Then perhaps it can be debated. Even better if the Federal Neighborhood Office was accepted into what will become part of Government 2.

CHAPTER 6. THE FEDERAL NEIGHBORHOOD OFFICE

The Federal Neighborhood Office (FNO) is a new kind of federal office. First, it is local. Second the FNO is the primary federal government customer service center. All government services for an individual are delivered through the FNO. The FNO is the customer service side of the Social Security Administration. The FNO also is the front office for a modernized United States Postal Service. The FNO is the customer service side of a new Internal Revenue Service. And it will be the local feature of other local federal offices. Basically, the FNO is the place to go for the local community to access federal services.

The size and locations of the FNO are based on the most recent census tracts. There were a bit over 70,000 census tracts in the 2010 census.[6] The FNO uses the census tract as the basis for the "neighborhood" it covers. Using census tracts the FNO has an average of about 4,000 people per FNO. The FNOs could range in size from 1200 to a bit over 8,000 residents. This book makes the assumption that there would be 1 FNO for

---

6 The precise number of FNOs is less a consideration, than an effective, externally validated objective method of subdividing the areas of the country to be most effective in not only efficiency, but also importantly, the ability for the public to identify, relate, and control their local operations, within the framework of federal law.

each census tract. It is very possible that a given FNO could support more than one census tract. That is one of the features of an FNO that would be proven during the Proof of Concept. The Proof of Concept is described in Volume 2 - Design and Implementation Planning (the second volume of the series).

Most FNO areas will have a physical building. But in some places, other options are needed. One example of that need is in Alaska. Alaska has an area called the Unorganized Borough. The unorganized borough has only a little over 80,000 people but is over 320,000 miles in area. That area is larger than any other state. That is basically 4 sq. miles per person. For that area a single building doesn't make a lot of sense. However, even in that part of Alaska there are a few towns like Bethel and Dillingham which are large enough to have a physical FNO. For most of that area, there is simply no population center which can operate as a focal point. These areas require a mobile FNO like a plane, helicopter, boat, or car which brings the essential portions of the FNO to the smaller communities on a scheduled basis. Also, each local FNO office has internet video capabilities along with VOIP for access from people's homes. That does assume that people have internet access which is unlikely in some cases, but very possible in other cases.

One of the ideas in Government 2.0 is recognizing that one size definitely doesn't fit all. As a result that means that funding for the site operations of the FNO has to be split from the actual delivery functions. That way fiscal controls are both effective and meaningful. This lets the FNO provide the local community with some input and control of the services that the federal government offers to the community. This then, allows community needs to be prioritized at the local rather than only at the federal or state level.

FNO OPERATIONS

The FNO has a few primary functions which are managed for the local community by a board. These are

- To provide a way to insure that federal services are made available on an equal basis

- To insure that the individual is supported in dealing with the federal government

- To provide the community a way to control local operations of the federal government

If we expect government to be fair, we need to have the same level of service given to everyone. This does not mean that everyone needs the same services. A retired person doesn't need the same things as a first grader. But the way that FNOs are organized, constructed, and finally began operations all need to be pretty much the same if we expect them to be able to offer the same level of service. That is also how we can make government services efficient. Some people think that only by making services be delivered more efficiently we will save money. This is probably not the case. Efficiency simply makes what we are doing get done quicker and easier.

It is not the efficiency however that results in the major cost savings. The cost savings comes by having the processes while standardized be optional in their application according to the individual who requires the service. We don't need to give the first grader the same things we expect government to do for a retiree. What we need is the right service at the right time for the right people. That decision capability is why we need to use private enterprise to contract with the federal government to fulfill these operations is the way it is done effectively, efficiently, and cheaper.

OPERATIONS STARTUP SUPPORT

Just about every single thing done by an FNO could and probably will be repeated at other FNOs over the next year. That is why standard processes are important. And with 70,000 FNOs to open there must even be a standard way of opening an FNO. To have that standard process, the Federal Information Service developed the initial series of manuals. They wrote a manual for the FNO board operations. They also had to write manuals for the service center operations. The FIS even needed to write manuals for things like the office support operations. You can read more about the FIS in Chapter 10.

The FIS is responsible for these manuals, adding and updating the manuals as needed. Most of the changes will be included with what is learned during the Proof of Concept described in Volume 2. That book also describes the installation of Pilot FNOs. The pilot FNOs will cause more updates to these manuals. These manuals are included as part of the Service Contract for the companies who provide the services to the FNOs. The Board Manual for example, contains critical dates for periodic activities such as dates that the local board needs to initiate vendor contract renewals. They also describe standard processes such as how to run board meetings. The idea is to provide the tools for the FNOs to be successful.

Remember, that most people who work at an FNO are not government employees. They are people who work for small companies who provide services to the FNOs. Not only the customer service functions, but facilities management functions (housekeeping, janitorial grounds services) and IT functions have multiple vendors who could provide the service to a single FNO. This lets the board choose the vendors they believe are most suitable to their needs, including local vendors who can submit bids as well.

When an FNO is first starting up the FIS will select the initial vendor who will manage the operations. That vendor will operate the FNO until a new board is established. The board then can let the first vendor continue to provide the service or they can decide that a new vendor is needed. The board can then award the service contracts to other vendors as they see the needs of the community.

STANDARD SERVICES

MAIL SERVICES

As FNOs open, local mail operations are taken over by the GAA selected by the FIS. They will first provide physical delivery services to the local FNO. Then as residents get Federal ID Cards and set up their PDS cards, email services will start. The GAA will also provide the other current services provided by the local post office.

SPECIAL NEEDS SUPPORT

Because each FNO is relatively small, not all services will need to be fully staffed at each FNO. However there are needs for specialty services. One example is that described in the Amish Story where the residents did not allow use of modern technology. GAA service contracts will be flexible enough that unique resident needs can be addressed. The standard process can allow for unique services, if that is needed, through specialty services.

CHANGE OF ADDRESS SUPPORT

Initially the FNO provides basic change of address support. As added functions are made available through the transition of the US Postal Service, more extensive Address Change processing will be added. This would include ties to State Elections Boards for those states which opt in for that function.

FEDERAL ADVOCATE FUNCTIONS

The FNO is designed to support the residents in dealing with the government. To do this, each FNO includes a Federal Advocate function. This function is to help the individual in dealing with various federal agencies who don't normally work with the general public. This could include agencies like the EPA. The Federal Advocate function is different from the FNO specialty services. The specialty service support is to help residents of the

FNO in using the procedures and processes. The Federal Advocate function is to be a voice for the resident. This function is to advocate for the residents. The emphasis for the FNO Advocate is to be on the side of the resident, not the agency.

WHO STAFFS THE FNO?

Staffing for the FNO actually comes from the contracts issued by the Federal Information System to start the deployment of each FNO. Those contracts are for services to be provided by local service vendors who are GAAs. After the startup period, the locally elected board of the FNO selects the FNO service vendors. The board selects these vendors from a service catalog. The service catalog contains GAAs for the FNO area.

There will always be service vendors for the following:

FACILITIES SERVICE MANAGEMENT

The use of local vendors for certain services only makes sense since there are going to be well over 50,000 FNOs. This would even be assuming that the number of FNOs was dropped by one third. Contracts like the one for Facilities Service Management provide for trash, cleaning etc. This is usually the first contractors to use local resources. Because the vendors recognized as a GAA for Service Centers need to keep their costs as low as possible, it large portion of GAA vendors will hire and train residents. This will build the vendor expertise to deliver effective FNO assistance.

TECHNOLOGY SUPPORT OPERATIONS

Another GAA for the FNOs is for Infrastructure Technical Support. These vendors provide all IT services needed by the FNO and the FNO residents' access to their PDS. This would include, PC replacement, virus scans, printer fixes.

SPECIALTY SERVICES VENDORS

Specialty service vendors can be used when a given FNO doesn't need a full time person. These vendors would also be GAAs. They would be able to provide either part time, or even virtual customer Service Representatives. Again, recognition that one size doesn't fit all, dictates what should be used for a given FNO. For example that an FNO on one of the Indian Reservations needs support for interacting with the Bureau of Indian Affairs, while an FNO in Brooklyn probably doesn't.

What vendors are needed is mostly determined by the needs of the local community. That in part is why the FNO board is important. They are the ones who determine what needs the neighborhood has. They also decide how much need there is for specialty services. This in turn will guide how many different kinds of specialty GAAs there are needed in the local area. The number, of different kinds of specialty GAAs depends on the effectiveness of the Federal Function Identification Program. This will determine the cost, how much variation is needed, and will also help to hold the Customer Service GAA costs down.

WHO RUNS THE FNO?

In technology we often build up a question like that into fancy terms. The group or board who manages the FNO is called the governance. Simply put, FNO governance is at two levels. The first level is the operational management of the FNO by the FNO Board. The second level is by the residents of the community who elect the FNO board.

FNO INSTALLATION MANAGER

The GAA setting up the FNO designates an Installation Manager. The Installation Manager is the person appointed by the GAA to handle opening and running the FNO at the beginning. The GAA who has the contract to set up the FNO is selected by the FIS. After the FNO is running normally, the FNO Board takes over running the FNO.

THE FNO BOARD

After the initial startup period for the FNO, an FNO board is elected. Each FNO has a board comprised of 5 individuals, four of the members are elected by the residents of the FNO. The 5th representative is chosen by the 4 members from a list of nominees submitted by the vendors who provide services to the FNO. This 5th board member representative only has a vote in the event of ties between the other 4 board members. Board members serve terms of 2 years. Board members can only serve 3 consecutive terms. Board members can be subject to recall through the FNO voting functions. Board members are responsible for the selection of all

vendors for the FNO after the initial setup period which
is managed by the FIS.

The FNO board has final authority on the selection of
vendors. They are the group who is responsible for the
effectiveness of the FNO. It is the board who decides on
the mix of specialty GAAs needed by the local
community.

FNO VOTING SYSTEM

The FNO has an online voting system. It is through this
system that the residents of the FNO vote on questions
placed by the board. The residents can also vote on
items put on the ballot by residents of the community.
The community could even vote on items added to the
ballot by local, state and federal officials who represent
the FNO. The voting system supports making the
decisions for the local area be set by the residents and
the FNO board.

Specific questions, such as recall of a board member
could require different majorities. The FNO voting
system could even be set to require different quorums.
These decisions would be set by legislation prior to the
FNOs start of operations.

Initially, many decisions can be made by the local
community using the voting system. This could include
the hours the FNO is open. It could even include the
name of the FNO. In addition, once all the FNOs are
running, Congress could easily pass legislation to
provide direct local funding to the FNO. That way, the
FNO would truly have more control over what is being
done on the local level.

However, the most important decision initially is who will be on the FNO board. It is the board who will manage the local operations. The FNO Electronic voting system provides the direct support needed by the FNO to handle the local board elections. Lastly, the FNO Electronic voting system provides the mechanism for the direct election of the Federal Local Magistrate who is part of the Federal Local Magistrate Board.

One question that will always be on the ballot standard is "Do you believe your management team is serving your best interests?" If at any voting period, a majority of those voting No exceeds 25% of the total residents, a new local FNO election will be held in the next election. This power to recall bad board members through anonymous voting is the most important feature of the Electronic Voting System.

CHAPTER 7. THE PERSONAL DATA STORE

The Personal Data Store (PDS) is the second of the three major additions to Gov 2.0. The PDS design improves the security of a person's data. That is because, the data is not housed in each agency separately, but where each person decides to store it. Because the data is now stored in one place, the owner not only keeps control but then has more stake in the security of the data. Just by itself, this helps to improve the security of the information.

The PDS becomes in effect a new way for government to store and retrieve a person's information. This allows the old way to be dropped. It also means that all of the government services that use the information have to be redesigned. This allows the service to be tailored and redefined to be more effective and efficient. In effect, technology from the PDS and the FNO provides a completely different way of using technology in Government.

So what is a PDS? The Personal Data Store is cloud storage. Just as important, it is a structured storage for each person. The PDS is a series of directories and folders sort of like the My Documents area of a personal computer. However, some of the folders and directories has very specific contents and formats. These directories and folders are a structured set of information about the person who owns the PDS. Every individual in the US will have his or her own unique folder. For ease of description, the PDS is generally called the individual's electronic home on the web. With a minimum of four separate root directories called wings the PDS when fully populated contains the primary data source for the government's information about the individual. Each wing has one or more rooms, with two of the wings being predefined.

The structuring of the information needed by the government makes make access and presentation of the information:

- Easy for the individual.

- Easy for the Government Authorized Agent (GAA) when needed.

- Easy to trace the actions of the GAA by the individual.

- Easy to move to other vendors as the individuals needs and preferences change.

- More secure than would be available in a series of centralized data stores within the federal government

The public room is essentially the front porch of a person's electronic house. It is there where visitors can retrieve your name, actual address, and some minimal general information about you. Most people and search engines can access this information. You could however, post a flag to show you want your information to be hidden. That flag could be checked by the normal search engines like Google or Yahoo. That same flag could be set to allow people to access your front porch information, but to track who actually retrieved your information.

THE GOVERNMENT WING

This wing of the individual's Electronic House contains several rooms.

The Government Information Room is where your interactions with the federal government are stored. It is always accessible by you. This is the place where your post office email mail is received, including what is currently some of the mail that comes in through the mailbox outside your real front door.

The Federal Government Wing also contains rooms for each Government agency that needs to maintain information about you. These rooms, for example, include the Social Security Room and the IRS room. All electronic information about you and used by the agencies would be kept in these rooms. You would be able to access these rooms at any point as well.

The Federal Archives room contains final copies of any tax returns. Once you are out of the armed forces, it will have your Selective Service record. It will also have your social security contribution history. It would contain a record that you voted in each FNO election. If you live in a state that participates in the Federal Election Voting System, your voting history would be kept there as well.

The Government Wing contains rooms for the States use along the same lines as the federal government. States would be able to use the PDS if:

a) The state joins the Personal Data Store Network (PDSN)   b) you authorize the use of the rooms by the state as well.

You PDS will also have a Control Room where you can manage your PDS. By manage we mean who can access what information in your PDS. It also includes the locations you can access your PDS. In addition, it includes what kind of ways you can access your PDS (cell phone, home PC, laptop). Lastly, it allows you to decide what information is allowed to each approved visitor. [7]

THE RECORDS WING

The Records Wing contains several rooms and documents as well. First, the Records Wing contains the Access Log. That is a record of every access of your PDS from any authorized organization or person. The Access Log includes a record of which rooms were accessed or denied based on who you want to allow looking into your rooms.

Your Personal Records room can have electronic copies of your birth certificate. If you want to keep an electronic copy of your passport, you could keep it there. You could even include copies of your permanent record from your school days. Basically, your Personal Records room has the information you need to be able to validate yourself.

---

[7] The Control Room is initially contained in the Government Wing for several reasons, the chief of which is that the room must exist even if the individual does not elect to pay for the Personal Wings of the electronic house. Immediately upon contracting to have a personal wing, the vendors would be expected to change the links to the control room to that contracted personal wing. In the event that the owner ceases to have a personal wing, the linkage would change back to the Government wing.

MEDICAL RECORDS WING

Your Medical Records wing contains exactly what you think it does. It has rooms that provide an electronic copy of your medical records. These rooms are similar to the federal rooms. You control access to which Physicians, hospitals etc. can update if you authorize them to do so. There will be at least one room for each physician and or hospital. Over time, this could replace the current physical medical records maintained by hospitals and physicians separately.

In concept, the Medical Records wing should have at least one room for each health care worker who has treated you. Doctors and hospitals would have to use this wing to update your medical records.[8] You should know that current electronic medical records are stored in a variety of formats that. What this means is that the records stored in your PDS could also have separate formats. Just like today, viewers would be available to see the information from any licensed vendor. [9] Interfaces could be available for the current electronic medical records systems. This would make it easier to help the staff load the information into the EMR more easily.

---

[8] Since it's expected to take between 3-7 years for most people to establish and begin to use their PDS, this would only apply to those who are using PDSs.

[9] Alternatively all medical records could be stored in a single standard format, and the vendors would have to translate their proprietary format into that standard. That is truly on an effort this size a technical detail for later.

To control the access to the personal EMR, the PDS owner would be able to set temporary usernames and passwords. Doctors and nurses could use these to access a patient's medical records. These passwords would be valid for only a given period of time. The purpose would be for the doctor or nurse to be able to access and update the medical record for their treatments or the physician's notes. It would also help in case of emergencies.

MEDICAL RECORDS EXCEPTIONS TO PRIVACY – ACCIDENTS

There are several circumstances that do however change that situation. Say you were brought in to an emergency room from an accident. The staff could override the security of your PDS and get into your EMR. It would however be logged as an unapproved access to your information. Assuming you were successfully treated, you would be able to review the access and their actions.

MEDICAL RECORDS EXCEPTIONS TO PRIVACY - GUARDIANSHIP

Sometimes, a guardian is appointed when you are unable to make decisions for yourself. When that happens, the appointed guardian(s) would be able to access your PDS. They also would likely be able to authorize medical staff to access your Medical Record History. This would help them to provide better treatment. Even though the guardian will have access to your PDS, it will NOT include the ability to vote in the FNO Voting System.

MEDICAL RECORDS EXCEPTIONS TO PRIVACY AND ACCESS – MENTAL HEALTH

There can be situations where the ability to access your medical information would not be in your best interests. In these circumstances, the physician could essentially order you a prescription. The prescription could be used by the FNO to set a semi-permanent password on his portion of your EMR. That way you would be denied access to his records during your course of treatment. This prescription would have to be provided to the patient before the record would be sealed. This would allow the physician to be both open in their records, and still make decisions based on the best interests of the patient.

EDUCATION WING:

If you were in school, there could be a room for each place you went to school, where you could see your permanent record. At least you could see it, if there is such a thing.

PERSONAL WINGS

The Individuals Electronic Home could also contain Personal Wings for many different sets of information. These wings also may be added costs from the vendor. Whether your PDS has these wings depend on who your vendor is. Vendors may well offer different options so some of these may not be available for all vendors. Remember, that the person can choose their vendor, and this is one of the ways vendors try to make themselves attractive to customers.

The Personal Wings can include your offices where you can maintain basic cloud storage.

A second Personal Control Room can control the access of all your personal rooms in the same way you control your government rooms

Social Media wings could initially be used to set up and maintain access to your social media. You could also establish family rooms where information for the family can be maintained, one or more friends room where information that you want to make available to your friends can be shared, and which can be made no longer sharable and can close the room if and when your BFF becomes your WEF (Worst Enemy Forever).

WHERE IS YOUR PDS

The flip answer is that the PDS is in the cloud. A more accurate answer is that it will be on servers managed by one of the licensed PDS vendors. Companies like Hewlett Packard, IBM, Verizon, Amazon, Google and others can apply for licenses to be a PDS vendor. The essence of the PDS vendor is that they are responsible for making sure your data is secure. This means secure not only in the sense of being backed up, but also in the sense of insuring that you have control of who accesses it. A licensed PDS Vendor is also responsible for insuring that the FIS standard format are used for the various Government wings. They are responsible to make sure your data is backed up. Lastly, they are responsible for insuring that every 1 access to your information is logged and reported to you.

WHO OWNS THE PDS

The PDS is legally owned by you. This also means that access to the PDS is controlled by you. That is, you have control over who gets access to it, which vendor manages it for you, and what features you want beyond the minimal rooms that comprise the government wing.

In the real world, you can "move" from one neighborhood to another. A similar feature will exist for your PDS. PDS vendors must supply features that will allow you to move your "home" to any another PDS vendor.

WHAT CONTROLS THE ACCESS TO THE PDS

Except for specific court orders, the simple answer is you do.

You can require a search warrant before your home can be entered. In the same way, you can control who accesses your information. Each room in your house will have secure access. This means you can control who is granted complete access, or who must "sign" for access, and who will only be granted guided access, that is, you will be able to see what information they access in real time.

Further details about how you can control the access to your PDS are found in Appendix D. You can also read more about what are the exceptions to your control, and how secure your PDS really is.

CHAPTER 8. THE FEDERAL LOCAL MAGISTRATE COURT

The FLMC is the third component of Gov 2.0. FLMC stands for Federal Local Magistrate Court. The FLMC is a significant addition to the current federal court system. Because the FLMC is an addition, more details about what are the changes to the existing court system is needed. Also, the parts of the judiciary that are new with the FLMC also needs to be described. That determines the role of the FLMC. In turn, that helps to describe how the FLMC influences and is impacted by the existing federal, state and administrative courts.

In order to understand the FLMC it helps to understand the current federal courts. Most people have no idea how the federal court system was structured when it was first put together. Simply put, it was based on one of the first bills passed by the first congress. In addition to the Supreme Court defined in the Constitution, there are also two additional levels of courts, the circuit court and the Appeals Court. These were first added as part of that bill. The name circuit court sounds funny today, but it was actually a very good description when that court was first started. In fact, the circuit court got its name because Supreme Court justices were expected to "ride" the circuit. The Supreme Court justices literally were meant to go from town to town hearing the cases that involved federal law. Over time, the number of each of these courts has grown, and a

few special purpose courts like bankruptcy court have
been added but the three-tier structure has been in
place practically since the beginning of the US. Can you
imagine one of the current Supreme Court judges doing
that today?

There is another significant piece of the federal court
that most people do not even realize exists. These are
called the administrative courts. These courts are not
even in the judicial branch of the government at all.
These are the courts that are part of the Executive
Branch. These courts handle cases like EPA regulation
interpretations. There are courts for civil rights cases.
There are courts for disability cases in the Social
Security administration. In fact, the size of the
administrative courts is far larger than the actual
federal judiciary. When you walk through the various
agencies, it seems like any agency that ends up having
rules to enforce about either people or companies
seems to have something that either is called a court, or
functions as a court.

The FLMC is a local court which handles the functions
covered by the administrative courts. It is a single court
system that is an addition to the existing federal courts.
In fact, it is one of the changed responsibility in the
circuit court to oversee these courts. This actually is
close to what appears to be the original intent of the
Constitution. In addition to the administrative law, the
FLMC also is the first court to which individuals can
direct their complaints. It provides a way for them to
have their rights protected. It also allows people to seek
redress when the federal agency is not acting in
accordance with its own rules.

Because of that, the FLMC is in effect a new kind of court.

EXTENDING THE FEDERAL COURTS

Since the country started, most changes in the Federal Courts have been to try to adjust the caseload of the court itself. Caseload increases come about first because of increased population. They also occurred because of the increased size of the country itself. The number of cases also grew because of new laws, including civil rights laws. Finally, increases in the scope of government and the court system itself caused more cases for the courts to hear. Most of these changes have occurred within both of the parallel systems of states and federal courts.

Very little has been done to address the cause of the increased cases in the system today. Instead, we have gone to a system of plea bargains for some cases, mediation for many contract law cases, and even arbitration for contracts. Indeed, it seems that the need to plea bargain is mostly a way to reduce the case burden on the system. That occurs even at the cost of infringing on a person's rights.

The unfortunate part of the way that the US Federal courts are set up is that they generally apply only to significant or publicized cases, not smaller cases. When a case is just about a single person, most people can't really use the court system because of the high cost, and long timeframes cases need to get through that system.

The FLMC is the biggest change to the federal court system since judges stopped riding the circuit courts. It is the most significant change because it is NOT intended to patch the existing structure. The FLMC replaces a large part of the existing law system in the executive branch. The FLMC is a local court with a better way of dispensing justice. In doing so, the FLMC helps to decentralize the federal government. And it will reduce the overall power of the executive branch over the individual.

The very existence of the FLMC makes if more likely to improve making justice more timely especially by taking advantage of current technology.

RELATIONSHIP OF THE FLMC TO THE FEDERAL NEIGHBORHOOD OFFICE

The small size of the FNOs makes the establishment and use of a Federal local small claims court practical. This is true for many of the administrative law cases. This includes such things as Social Security hearings and IRS hearings. Unlike the administrative courts, the FLMC can provide not only an initial hearing, but in most cases it can resolve the case more quickly. The FLMC is better able to provide real mediation with streamlined procedures not just a push to get the case closed. This will not only stream line court procedures but it will improve the speed at which regulations are enforced.

The FLMC is not intended to replace or override local state law. The FLMC is intended to cover the gaps as far as rights issues. By moving these types of cases to local courts, and hence in front of the public, where it is appropriate justice can be more rapidly achieved.

STRUCTURE OF THE FEDERAL LOCAL MAGISTRATE COURTS

There are about 600 Federal Magistrate Judges (FMJ) in the Federal Judiciary. That means that there would be under 120 FNOs per FMJ. While FMJs are not organized directly by census tracts, census tracts do not overlap Congressional district boundaries. That means that a given set of FNOs can be grouped under a single FMJ. That in turn means that a given FLMC could always be assigned to a specific FMJ as well. Even though it is unlikely that all FLMCs would be equally apportioned among magistrates it would be pretty close.

All of this means that there would be 1 FLMC for every 20,000 people or for every 5 FNOs.

The operations of the FLMC are meant to be extremely limited. Because of that, the FLMCs need to run just on a part time basis. From a structural standpoint, the FLMC would appear like the following:

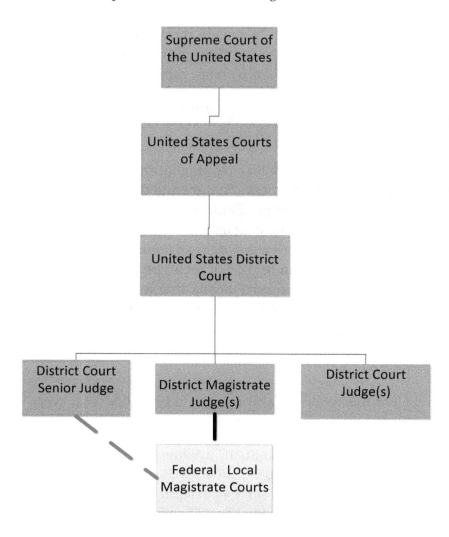

The dotted line relationship to the most Senior Judge within the federal district is explained in that the Senior Judge is involved when there is a need to remove a sitting local magistrate.

More details about the FLMC can be found in Appendix E. There you can find out how cases are filed. You can also read about FLMC limits on rulings and appeals. There you will find how magistrates are shared, and how they are initially appointed. Finally you can read about the qualifications and term of the FLM and the Chief Magistrate.

CHAPTER 9. WHY ARCHITECT GOV 2.0 THIS WAY

I have been asked, "When do you actually start working on an Enterprise Architecture?" The easy answer is when you meet the customer or manager. Enterprise architecture is very formal in some ways. Enterprise architecture can have very formal results. Initially though designing an architecture begins as pulling ideas and thoughts together. These thoughts get organized into structures. The structures are rearranged again, and again, and again. At best from an architectural viewpoint, this book is really trying to describe a work effort that is at this initial stage.

As I edited the book the size of this chapter continued to grow, to the point where I split it in three. Perhaps, that is a sign that there is a need for changes, or perhaps I simply run off my mouth at a keyboard. The split is along the lines of the major drivers from outside the system as it exists today (this chapter). What follows are the drivers from what are weaknesses in the system as it exists today (Chapter 10). The last portion is the drivers from the perspective of the major components added with Government 2.0 (Chapter 11). I hope this makes the ideas somewhat more readable.

WHY DID YOU INCLUDE .... ?

It is elusive to describe how those initial thoughts slowly change. The thoughts evolve into something more and more coherent. From experience architects and designs know that it won't be perfect the first time, or perhaps even the tenth time. This is especially true when there is no peer review, no formal work sessions, and no work product review except those who are have been reading drafts. Nevertheless, this chapter contains some of the reasoning that led to those components you have read about in the preceding chapters.

Generally, some parts of a general design, even a high-level visionary design are obvious only to the original designer. Sometimes, things can appear purely arbitrary. When designs and architectures are reviewed, this is where most of the time is spent. Reviewers ask why you had this function. Why didn't you add this other function? Who decided that something should be stored and how did you come to this decision? Why is it this way and not that way? Sometimes some pieces can appear to be purely arbitrary, even if the reasoning is legitimate. To be blunt though, there are times when some pieces can be purely arbitrary.

Sometimes, a system is so big, that some parts that could be included are not. It gets decided that an area that could be part of the system is excluded. It happens simply to let the design concentrate on those functions that he thinks are more important, this allows him to exclude those portions that could be done later.

Usually some of the biggest questions regard why some areas were ignored or intentionally excluded. The one intentionally excluded are in the next section. The other reason some pieces are ignored is that they simply were missed.

Then there are the big pieces and the little pieces that ARE part of the architecture. The big pieces become the primary drivers of the strategic design process. The biggest primary driver is the need to handle something new. More about these new requirements is in Chapter 13.

The remainder of this chapter provides a description of the primary drivers and the component design reasons

Primary drivers also included for Gov 2.0:

- Change to size of User base:
- Technology Change itself including
  o New storage or communications capabilities, new design frameworks
  o Completely new technologies
- Aged Systems which can no longer be changed

These in turn drive some of the more significant structural design features

- Why is so much of the existing structure of the federal agencies changed?
- Why are new structures needed?

These design features in the end drove some of the most significant visible changes to the structure of Government 2.0 that answers the following truly basic questions that are covered in the final sections of this chapter.

Why a PDS?

Why have an FNO at all?

Why have a FIC?

Why have the FIS?

Why have the FLMC?

WHY DID YOU NOT INCLUDE ....

There are several areas that were intentionally left out of the scope of Gov 2.0. These included

NATIONAL DEFENSE

The Department of Defense (DOD) was excluded for several reasons. First, most of the DOD isn't involved in delivering services to people. Second, the pieces that do get involved in delivering services to people are already separated. The VA is the one obvious example. The VA is a service delivery organization. As a result it has been included in the scope of Gov 2.0.

The third reason is more complex. Decentralizing the operations of the federal government is one of the core principles of this book. This very idea places a large burden on the DOD to support the transition. This in effect becomes an added long-term burden while continuing to provide support for the defense of the country as a whole. Protecting those assets of the federal government while they are being decentralized in effect places a hidden but significant burden on the defense agencies **while** the overall transition is occurring.

Once transforming government has reached the point where it has its own momentum, then perhaps the DOD changes can be reexamined. Then the DOD would benefit from doing the same thing as was done to the non-DOD agencies. So the recommendation is to take on those changes later.

NATIONAL SECURITY AGENCIES

The National Security Agencies were also dropped from Gov 2.0. Why? For the same reasons that applied to the DOD.

Just like the DOD there is an exception for national security as well. The exception is in regards to everyone's privacy. The ideas described as part of the PDS chapter and the PDS Appendix apply to the National Security agencies just like every other organization. This is true for notices and court orders.

STATE AND LOCAL GOVERNMENT FUNCTIONS

It would have been very easy to extend the scope Government 2.0 into the states.

However, Gov 2.0 is a federal initiative. All of the services and functions of Gov 2.0 must first occur at the federal level. That is where the changes will be legislated and implemented. The constitution limits what the federal government can do. This is especially true on what changes it can force on the states. While the concepts could be applied to state and local government, these were kept out of the scope. Why? Because the need for the changes is greatest at the federal government level.

You may have noted that in the description and indeed the systems designs, the participation of the states would be at each state's discretion. That method of description is essentially because the federal government cannot impose its will on the states for those types of activities. The same reasoning applies to local government functions as well.

WHY NOT RE-DESIGN THE POSTAL BRANCHES AS THE FNO.

Re-engineering the local postal branch into the FNO was discarded as an option. Here's why.

The population size of the service area of each local post office varies a lot. That means different FNOs would be of drastically different sizes. This would mean that different levels of resources would be needed from community to community, even within the same function.

It has been a major political problem whenever closing postal branches is attempted. FNOs are dependent on the size and scope of census tracts. Using these objective groupings should reduce that specific issue.

The local post offices are a creation of the Postal Service as a whole and managed as a part of that whole. Making the branches dependent on a local board would be a difficult process.

The current USPS culture is based on centralized decision-making and local execution. It has no history that supports local control.

As a result, despite the apparent costs, creating the FNOs seemed the better option, than the risks which would need to be handled in evolving the USPS branches.

POPULATION DRIVERS OF GOVERNMENT 2.0

In 1790, there were under 4 million people in the US. This was the population base when the Constitution was ratified.

Here is the population by State as of the 1790 census[10]

District	Free white males of 16 years and upward, including heads of families.	Free white males under 16 years.	Free white females, including heads of families.	All other free persons.	Slaves.	Total.
Vermont	22,435	22,328	40,505	255	16a[.] b[.]	85,539

District	Free white males of 16 years and upward, including heads of families.	Free white males under 16 years.	Free white females, including heads of families.	All other free persons.	Slaves.	Total.
New Hampshire	36,086	34,851	70,160	630	158	141,885
Maine	24,384	24,748	46,870	538	0	96,540
Massachusetts	95,453	87,289	190,582	5,463	0	378,787
Rhode Island	16,019	15,799	32,652	3,407	948	68,825
Connecticut	60,523	54,403	117,448	2,808	2,764	237,946

District	Free white males of 16 years and upward, including heads of families.	Free white males under 16 years.	Free white females, including heads of families.	All other free persons.	Slaves.	Total.
New York	83,700	78,122	152,320	4,654	21,324	340,120
New Jersey	45,251	41,416	83,287	2,762	11,423	184,139
Pennsylvania	110,788	106,948	206,363	6,537	3,737	434,373
Delaware	11,783	12,143	22,384	3,899	8,887	59,094 c[ꞏ]
Maryland	55,915	51,339	101,395	8,043	103,036	319,728

District	Free white males of 16 years and upward, including heads of families.	Free white males under 16 years.	Free white females, including heads of families.	All other free persons.	Slaves.	Total.
Virginia	110,936	116,135	215,046	12,866	292,627	747,610
Kentucky	15,154	17,057	28,922	114	12,430	73,677
North Carolina	69,988	77,506	140,710	4,975	100,572	393,751
South Carolina	35,576	37,722	66,880	1,801	107,094	249,073
Georgia	13,103	14,044	25,739	398	29,264	82,548

District	Free white males of 16 years and upward, including heads of families.	Free white males under 16 years.	Free white females, including heads of families.	All other free persons.	Slaves.	Total.
Total	807,094	791,850	1,541,263	59,150	694,280	3,893,635

∧ **a:** The census of 1790, published in 1791, reports 16 slaves in Vermont. Subsequently, and up to 1860, the number is given as 17. An examination of the original manuscript shows that there never were any slaves in Vermont. The original error occurred in preparing the results for publication, when 16 persons, returned as "Free colored," were classified as "Slave."

∧ **b:** Corrected figures are 85,425, or 114 less than the figures published in 1790, due to an error of addition in the returns for each of the towns of Fairfield, Milton, Shelburne, and Williston, in the county of Chittenden; Brookfield, Newbury, Randolph, and Strafford, in the county of Orange; Castleton, Clarendon, Hubbardton, Poultney, Rutland, Shrewsburg, and Wallingford, in the county of Rutland; Dummerston, Guilford, Halifax, and Westminster, in the county of Windham; and Woodstock, in the county of Windsor.

The table includes a breakdown which reflects society as a whole. Note the footnote about Vermont. The census even included Kentucky, Vermont and Maine as a separate census districts. These three states were not yet states in 1790.

Compare that to the US Population in 2010, which was 308 million people. That means the population is now over 75 times larger.

It's hard to understand how much the country has grown. Here are some things that may help. The Northwest Territories were to get a territorial legislature when its population GREW to 5,000 white adults. This didn't happen until 1798. The Northwest Territory was big. It eventually became several states. These were Ohio, Indiana, Michigan, Wisconsin, Illinois, and even a small piece of Minnesota. Those states now each have more than 50 million people. That's more than 10,000 times larger than that original territorial legislature.

Today 26 states have more people than the entire country in 1790.

TOWN HALL CONCEPTS

One of the interesting features of representative government is the concept of town hall meetings. These were scheduled meetings in towns and villages in New England states. Town halls let residents bring up their concerns. In some locations the townspeople actually voted on issues brought before the town board.

The town halls worked particularly well when the population was homogeneous and not too large. Town halls generally faltered badly when populations grew too large.

POPULATION SIZE CONSTRAINTS

Some of the proposals in this book could apply to all levels of government. However, the constitution was a contract between the states and the federal government. It wasn't a contract between the people and the states, or between the government and the towns. Changing components of the federal government doesn't force the changes to other levels of government. Wherever possible, the systems and processes provided in government 2.0 do not exclude states from doing the same thing. The states could even integrate these ideas further. However, this would be at the discretion of each state. Basically, the framework of Government 2.0 is that, if you build it, they will come.

TECHNOLOGY DRIVERS OF GOVERNMENT 2.0

FROM QUILL AND PEN TO THE CLOUD

When you compare systems today with the systems of 1790, it's easy to think that there is no comparison. Technology itself was very different from what we think of as technology today. The state of the art in 1790 was quill and paper for recording. Communications was at the speed of the printing press. The printing press was used for distributing ideas, decisions, requests for inventory etc. etc. etc. The only dynamic storage media at that time was the human brain and the chalkboard.

Today it is a different world. If you are looking to re form a government it is not the functions that government performs that must change. What must change is the way it performs those functions. That change is actually at the heart of the redesign effort.

From a cursory review, the federal government has only a couple of really basic services to provide.

These include

> Defense of the country, [11]
> Creation and enforcement of the laws,
> Providing services to the population,
> Collecting revenue to pay for the above.

The way you could use technology was limited in the pre-1800 world. Technology was not equally available at all places either. Everything in the government was managed from one location because each small addition to the government was most easily done that way. Big government didn't get to be large overnight, it was small changes added a bit at a time.

Today we have an industry called government.

The people who were employed to provide these common services thought of each agency as a separate part of the whole, defined to deliver or protect a basic function of government.

As each agency grew, it began to run like a separate business. Virtually identical services were built and operated within each agency. After a certain point, as

---

[11] Defense of the country has been intentionally excluded from the scope of Government 2.0 but is referenced here solely so be as comprehensive as possible

services were added, they were duplicated within an agency. Why? Because in part the agency itself defined the scope. Larger scopes required more funding. Funding is by agency. As it became obvious that there was power in managing these agencies it became even more unlikely that agencies would share a service.

Agency structures now always include several things. They include a group who defines the agency policy. These policies are supposed to reflect the law, but there are many examples where they do not. It did not start that way. Originally, agencies had a person, perhaps two people who translated the policy into procedures. This function grew until there was a small group who did the same thing. This group then grew into groups to the point where sometimes the groups themselves were duplicated within a single agency. To make sure that the policies were enforced the groups then duplicated not only the procedures, but also added people who checked to be sure the policy was enforced. In some agencies these are called auditors. In other agencies, they are called Quality Assurance. These people now are checking the people who actually were responsible for the service.

As the population and the country grew, the need to store large quantities of data grew as well. Even more there was a need to get at the data easily. Surprisingly, this helped to speed the early days of automation and computers, making things operate far faster and better. These first computers reduced some duplications as people modified the process. But. It also caused duplications as people were hired to check the new systems.

In other ways the computer operations mirrored the old manual system. They too were built as centralized systems. The computer operations in some ways became mirrors of the old processes. The last step has now occurred in that the delivery system now becomes a driver of the overall government as well.

The neural network and capabilities of today's systems do not require that centralized computing power. In fact today we can decentralize the information. Today we can separate the processes. We can redesign and change how things are done. Systems can be made easier to change.

Advanced network architectures not only allow these things, but also actually work better because of it. This is true so long as a couple of basic items are true. One is that rules for the decisions to be made are clearly defined. Another is that the decisions are clearly described. And the last is that the variations in decisions must be able to be repeated.

Today the concept of services is very important in systems design. Services begin as very small features and functions. You can combine these small services together into larger services. This allows designers to reuse the services and even to combine services reducing duplicated services. These services can combine into larger and larger services. Not only the smallest level service but also the large services lets developers use standards to ask for the service. Developers tend to call the standard way a protocol. Using these protocols, requests can be made within a system, or even across systems. This idea has had different names over the years. The current buzzword is

Service Oriented Architecture (SOA). SOA tends to fit the necessary models to support evolving the federal government services. The benefits of doing this is proportional to the size of the organization. Because the US Federal Government is so large, the benefits would be enormous.

From that beginning in the commercial side, the larger and larger concepts of services have been expanded to where you can now contract for buzzwords just like an IT geek. You can get SAAS. PAAS or IAAS right out of the vendors electronic portal. Just in case you were wondering SAAS is Software As A Service (for an entire application). PAAS is Platform As A Service (for entire operating systems. IAAS is Infrastructure As A Service for middleware like databases (), and other support function.

Make no mistake, these changes in systems design were done with multiple objectives, but for the most part they came down to the need for greater capabilities that developers saw, the need to overcome the limitations of single point of failure systems, and of course the need to get technology changes more quickly available to the customer.

While whole books could be written about the differences between the development models of government at the state, local and federal levels compared to the private sector, let us just agree they are different.

To achieve the benefits of things like SOA and the advanced technologies such as "the Cloud", the fundamental components of existing agencies will need

to transition to the service model, a process that will
not occur overnight, nor be easy.

STORAGE EVOLUTION FROM PUNCH CARD TO THE CLOUD

Before 1960 one of the advanced technologies was the
punch card. Some readers may not even know what a
punch card is, but Wikipedia had a good description.

"Now obsolete as **a** recording medium, punched cards
were widely used throughout the 19th century for
controlling textile looms and in the late 19th and early
20th century for controlling fairground organs and
related instruments. Punched cards were used through
most of the 20th century in what became known as the
data processing industry; the use of unit record
machines, organized into data processing systems, for
data input, processing, and storage.[1] Early digital
computers used punched cards, often-prepared using
keypunch machines, as the primary medium for input
of both computer programs and data.

Wikipedia itself says that these were obsolete. But as of
2012, some voting machines still utilize punched cards
to record data. That is after the 2004 election.
Remember Chad?

The punch card as a data storage media was replaced
by disk drives. These started out as large boxes, a bit
larger than a standard desk. These drives were set up
as needed with some data centers having acres of disk
drives. These drives were attached to larger and larger
computers all operating in a single room to process the
data. This was such a large process, that in one case,

they found the disk drives were too far from the computer. The distance caused the computers to have trouble getting the data because of the time delay. That is how big the data centers had become that even with data traveling at the speed of light (186,000 miles per second) computer rooms were too big. That particular problem was solved by putting disk drives on floors above and below the main computer. You can guess how costly that was.

The use of the punch card as an entry system began to be replaced with the advent of online systems. The widespread use of computer printers allowed the elimination of an entire type of device which is now almost completely eliminated. It is called unit record equipment. Unit record equipment was able to read the cards, and print directly on the top of the card the information stored in the card. Fancier pieces of this kind of equipment would read two cards and print information on a third card. The only place I am aware that still uses punch cards at all was in government. Why? Because it did not have to be efficient or effective.

Between 1970 and today, the transition from cards to a single location storage was first frantically fast, then it slowed, even as the ways we used data to protect the systems grow. Initially, backups were on punched cards. Then they were put on disk on those big box drives. We then changed to keep the data at a remote site, then finally to hot backups. Today we have distributed data storage. This process of moving to distributed data storage continues at an ever-faster pace. Why, because it is faster and cheaper.

The real benefit of being able to virtualize processes in the SOA models relies on being able to transition the information to be processed to a distributed environment as well.

Everything I have just described was really a complex way of saying that computer data is moving to "the Cloud". From a practical standpoint, the location of the data is no longer important. Multiple vendors provide storage and computing power via the cloud; with the consumer have no idea where the storage actually resides, just that they can get to it when they need to.

FROM BLACKBOARD TO DESKTOP, TO TABLETS

In 1790 the printing press was THE current technology. Another huge change was something called computing power. Computing power is how quickly a computer can execute an instruction. An instruction is a very small action on the part of a computer. You usually need many instructions put together for a computer to actually do anything. The only real computing power in 1790 was the human brain. Today we talk about computers being better chess players than people are. People IM and work in virtual meeting rooms. Emails are the normal way of communicating with leaving a record. This certainly wasn't true when the Republic was founded.

In 1790 the way to share ideas and quickly change them when working together was the blackboard. The blackboard serves as type of computing power. It allowed people to share and revise an idea until it was "right".

Today we have gone from punch cards to control fabric looms. We've taken the punch card and used it to store data with unit record equipment. We've taken the data on those and processed it. We progressed from Eniac which was among the first programmable computers to today. We now have IPhones, Ipads, Nooks, MS Surface, and Tablets provide more computing power that was even conceived back in 1970 much less 1790.

The first time I was a DP manager the company had a computer called the 370-115. It was the size of a larger standalone double freezer. It plus 4 drives, a printer, a card reader, and a cardpunch machine took up most of the space in a 25 x 25 foot room. It had 128K worth of memory. It cost about $125,000 for just the computer. Ten years later when I worked at a hospital, as a joke we laid out memory chips on a desk. We have room on a desk to have 16 times more than what that first computer could do. And memory was cheap enough that we could do that as a joke. Today, my cell phone has almost about 16,000 times more memory, and cost about $200.

We have reached the point where the actual machine used to access the information, is less important than that the access occur in a predefined consistent manner, and the format of the information has even to a degree become self-describing (although less than most developers really think).

Today we have browser-based systems. These are systems where the processing is spread across an environment. For example data retrieval from databases is controlled by one subsystem (generally called an RDBMS). Something called middle ware controls the application. It uses such things as rules engines, and encapsulated service objects. Security can be controlled by still other technologies. Buzzwords such as SSO (Single Sign On), and IDM (Identity Management System) are used to describe features which are used to control hacking.

And precisely NONE of this was anticipated in the federal government envisioned by the founders.

CHAPTER 10.   AGING FEDERAL SYSTEMS

MAKING A PATH TO THE FUTURE FOR AGING FEDERAL SYSTEMS

Behind the screen what you see in many government systems today was designed in the 1960s. These systems started running in the 60s and 70s and still run today. As mentioned in the intro to the book, redesigning computer systems is hard, really hard. That is why things like Services Oriented Architecture evolved in the first place.

Private companies use portals to access their HR. They have web front ends to see the order catalog. They use apps to create the bills for the customers. They provide their services through the cloud. In the 1960s company data processing was very much like government data processing. Today that is no longer true.

To get to way they do things today, most companies ended up creating new structures. They used many different kinds of technologies including tools like SharePoint. Once they had things running on those new architectures they moved functions and users to the new platforms over time.

Basically, they did not renovate the old software, they built a new home for the functions. Then they moved processes function-by-function into the new framework. When the replacements were fully functional, they junked the old systems.

A similar thing will have to occur with the Federal Government if we are to be able to transition technologies into the 21st century for the federal government

OPERATIONAL MODEL CHANGES FROM 1789 TO TODAY

The term Secretary was the term used for the person responsible for a federal agency when the government was started. We still use that term today. In 1789, the word secretary meant an assistant who was in charge of confidential information. That is because the agencies were so small. Today we think of agencies in terms of huge enterprise level operations (like the Commerce department). These large agencies did not exist when the country was founded.

In 1789 the Secretary perhaps a small staff, perhaps not. It needed a secretary because a department was not as a large operation. But each agency needed to be run by a trusted confidant.

Today as the government has grown, the functions of cabinet secretaries have grown as well. One big reason was that the government became a method of getting services to people. This is true whether it is a state or a federal agency. The growth patterns of state and federal agencies are the same.

As each agency grew, the structure remained the same. That is, each agency stayed as a hierarchy. Most of this hierarchy was concentrated in one spot. This has resulted in pushing all the authority to the top, along with ever-increasing loss of efficiency and productivity.

Thinking back to the very high-level service delivery model, there are certain benefits to the separation of responsibilities for each of the services, specifically

- Services tend to be more clearly defined when they are not treated as a singular process. This tends to elongate the lifespan of the service as well as making easier to apply because entire systems do not need to be changed. This then has the added benefit of being more flexible.

- Separating control functions from delivery functions usually helps to improve how well each function works. This is especially true when each service has separate success criteria. It is even more likely when each service also has separate reporting structures. Whether those services are automated or manual doesn't matter. What is important is that each service or function has a clear result. It is the quality of the result that matters most. Second is how effective the process was in getting the result, and only third is whether the process is efficient.

- Separation of services at the macro level allows for multiple processors. The term processors is used because the process could be performed either by a person or by a computer. When multiple processors are properly separated it is easier to compare the quality of service. The same is true for cost, and performance. In part, that is why making services sized so that larger number of companies can offer the service, drives innovation. It also improves efficiency. Moreover, it has the same effect on cost. This in brief is competition and it is possible in the government space.

• Keeping services separate also helps keep power from growing within an agency

In part, it was these considerations that drove the Functional Cataloging of the Federal Service functions.

WHY SO MUCH CHANGE TO EXISTING AGENCIES DESIGN

The size of the change in the agencies and departments of the Federal Government is large. The scope of these changes crosses agencies, divisions, and even party loyalties. But these changes did not come from a "blow the government up" approach. Instead, the changes, drastic as they appear, is due to just a few significant factors.

SERVICE ORIENTED DELIVERY SYSTEMS

Organizations which run as a single set of processers don't work well in distributed systems. This is especially true when they are managed from a single spot. Where that single location actually is, does not matter. In this case the spot is Washington DC. The real point is that to achieve a SOA approach, processes need to be split. The benefits of driving the customer facing functions out to the customer (the citizens) is obvious. The functional cataloging of the services was needed to allow that concept to be delivered. The delivery of that idea provides the opportunity to eliminate large sets of redundant functions across agencies. This in turn cuts costs and improves performance.

DECENTRALIZATION

Some people now think of the federal government as a separate entity. They believe that the federal government is not concerned about them. To a certain extent, they believe that the federal government is antagonistic to their hopes and dreams. To those folks it is the government which a threat. Whether they are 5% or 70% of the population is not important, what is important is that they believe government is the problem. President Reagan won office on essentially that theme.

What is even more telling is that there are people in government who believe that these same people are a threat to the government. They believe as the government, that they have the responsibility to keep these people from being in power. Again whether the number is 5% or 70% of government employees is not the point. The point is that these people should not have the power to act in a way which denies anyone their rights.

The core of the problem is not what the ideas are. The core of the problem is that the government should never exercise power to deny anyone's rights.

You simply cannot have freedom from the government when the government gets to decide what you are allowed to say. Even if you think that what they are saying is complete drivel. So long as we have the concentration of authority being increased even slowly in any one group of people, the awful chance grows that those people will abuse either the power, or worse abuse the people who they disagree with.

So what has this to do with decentralization? It actually has a lot to do with the issue in two separate ways. First, any of the changes needed to evolve governmental structures to become more effective will require pressure from some large portion of the American people. These people are likely to have these ideas attacked by those in the central bureaucracy.

The amount of power which is centralized today in what is called "inside the beltway" is huge. Any action which is taken to decentralize that power is a threat to those who act as if they have the right to decide what the proper role for government is. Decentralizing the government will cause this power to be reduced. This will be a struggle, but it is necessary.

Without bringing the services to the people, in a manner they understand effective change cannot occur. Bringing government to people as a service should begin to restore their belief in government. Without those changes in belief and effectiveness the country will not prosper or grow or perhaps even survive.

There is also a second architectural reason for decentralization.

In a broad sense, Washington is a single point of failure. Problems in its operation and processes disrupt if not cause breaks in the entire system. This weakness is being played out on the evening news.

OPERATIONS – EVOLVE OR SUPPLANT

There are times when a technologist looks at a system, and comes to the conclusion that the system needs to be redesigned. We are at that stage with the executive branch agencies. Redesign will result in the kinds of change described throughout the book.

HARDENING OF THE PROCESSES IN THE OLD SYSTEMS

Like the hardening of the arteries in the elderly processes can be clogged. This sometimes happens because they become so much a part of the organization that the purpose of the process gets lost. You can tell that this has happened when the people who execute the process don't remember the original purpose. This is when you hear comments like "This is what has always been done". The tendency to think in terms of what was always done becomes an obstacle to change. And more, this view becomes an opponent of making any changes at all.

In those instances, companies often go the route of complete replacement of a system. In severe cases companies have set up entire subsidiaries just to get out from under the weight of the "old school" processes. A case in point was the Saturn Corporation. Saturn was a spin off to attempt to build a new kind of car company from the ground up.

There are agencies in the US government today that are in this type of situation. These include the US Postal Service, The Internal Revenue Service, and the Veterans

Administration. The purpose remains valid. The process cannot be fixed, it must be replaced.

CURRENT STATE OF IT CONTRACTING AND PROCUREMENT IN THE FEDERAL SPACE

There are dozens if not hundreds of books on the federal government contracting and acquisition processes. These books identify multiple problems and propose solutions to fix federal contracts. Why? Simply put, federal buying has gotten too complex. It has gotten so complex, that multiple industry groups exist just to lobby about the process itself. They lobby to make sure each company gets a piece of the federal spending pie.

Underneath the paperwork, and the involved procedures there is a simple result. Because the process has been made so complex, there are only a few vendors who can even effectively bid on contracts. You see federal IT contracting is now as complicated as the federal tax code. Like the federal tax code it does not work well. I strongly believe that is true of most federal buying and spending The reason only a few vendors win bids, is because the rules assumes a winner take all structure to most projects.

Here are just a few of the ways Government 2.0 will affect federal buying.

PROJECT SPLITTING

Government IT projects can be huge. The larger the project, the more competition for the bid is needed. That competition creates risks that companies will lost federal funding. To counteract this, sometimes when multiple vendors are involved the government splits a project into segments. That way each vendor gets a piece of the pie. Different vendors takes leads in different parts of the effort. Each portion is still awarded on a winner take all approach. The core problem with this is we now have multiple federal contracts for one company to provide the design, while for the build component; they are specifically **excluded** from being able to bid **because** they did the design. Put simply, the folks who best understand how things were to be built are specifically told they cannot build it.

Why do companies like Verizon, HP, IBM, Northup Grumman, United Technologies, and so on, spend as much time and dollars lobbying to design the legislation as they do designing the systems. The answer is simple. Billions of dollars are won or lost on the way the contracts are defined, even before they are sent out to bid.

WHY CONTRACT WITH SO MANY COMPANIES WHEN YOU HAVE IDIQ

Having a large number of companies who can provide the same service makes it easier to pick vendors based on the quality of their service. While the culture of going to the lowest bidder, the actual focus should be on the best bidder. Best bidder is the one who has the right combination of price, quality, and service.

There are big advantages to having many companies provide the service. The problem with monopolies is obvious. Less obvious is when it is only a few companies get to sell their products. This is especially true when each company uses political power to get a part of the federal spending pie. This is yet another of the problems we have today. Today a purchasing method called IDIQ (Indefinite Delivery Indefinite Quantity Contracts) is often used. The idea with IDIQ is avoid picking a single winner. This in turn avoids having contract protests by the losing companies. These protests cost both time and money. IDIQ was an attempt to get protests to be less common. IDIQ contracts allows for multiple vendors to develop the same service or product. IDIQ would seem to fix the problem of a "winner take all" buying system.

Unfortunately, IDIQ does not fix much of anything. With IDIQ the problem becomes that those same "winners" are guaranteed that the company will definitely sell a minimum amount of the items. Quality, and effectiveness are more concept than reality. Competition may seem important in government buying, but the reality is that it is power which decides the winners.

Having many companies be able to sell the same service by itself won't fix the problem. Having, the people who use the service decide which companies sell a good product will.

MINORITY HELD BUSINESS DRIVERS

The idea of having minority businesses being guaranteed some portion of the federal pie was done with good intentions. The problem is that no contract is ever with a social group. Ever. Contracts are with people and companies. Even if the person is a handicapped minority business owner, the business sometimes is huge. It is power which matters in DC. I have worked for a minority held business which was run by an East Indian naturalized citizen. The company itself was 90% WASP. However, it met the criteria. Many companies are exactly like that simply to meet the federal rules to be sure to get a piece of that pie

.The concept of having minority business set aside contracts or requiring their use as a subcontractor is another example of the best of intentions paving the road to hell.

What makes it worse is employees in minority businesses are paid about the same as in non-minority businesses. Yet minority business were able to charge rates slightly higher than the non-minority counterpart businesses. This slight difference went straight to the bottom line of these companies. That would be OK, except that it has zero of the intended social benefits.

Bottom line, minority owned businesses do NOT materially benefit minorities, nor the government and actually cost more. This is why minority set-asides were not designed in the re-engineering of the delivery model in Government 2.0.

GOVERNMENT CONTRACTING CHANGE DRIVERS

What can work has been done on multiple occasions in the private sector.

ITIL formerly known as the Information Technology Infrastructure Library, is a set of practices for IT service management (ITSM) that focuses on aligning IT services with the needs of business. It was that concept that was used to develop the government service catalog. The idea of a government service catalog drives the changes to federal contracting.

Industry groups can work with organizations and the government to design the same kinds of standard interface for all electronic services. Vendors can then build the service to match the interface specification. The government or a standards group confirms that the service matches both the interface and the goal of the service. The vendor then sets pricing for the service and add it to what is called a service catalog. Small operations like the FNOs can then select from any number of vendor from the catalog. That way they can get the services they need perhaps even from people within the neighborhood. This in turn helps with both the decentralization of government and the delivery of more effective solutions.

CHAPTER 11. DRIVERS OF THE NEW ARCHITECTURE

DRIVERS OF THE PDS

DUPLICATION OF DATA

The amount of individual data currently under the control of the Federal government is huge. There is a cost to keep that data. The cost is not just in terms of actual storage, but also the effort it takes to keep the information accurate. There is also cost of backing up the information, getting it archived etc. This data is duplicated by agencies large and small. Some cost benefits will be gained by just placing each person's information into a single data structure. By getting rid of duplicate data we make it easier to track and keep the single copy of the data safe. It also makes it easier to improve the data accuracy.

Remember that we are talking about data structures not data storage. There is a difference between the two. Data structure is how the information is organized. Data storage describes where the information is stored.

The cost of both security and privacy rises in direct proportion to the number of copies of the information that are kept. The ability to control access to that information while individually is less, because of that redundancy gets larger very quickly.

PRIVACY CONSIDERATIONS

The European Union courts is struggling to handle requests for people to be unlisted on the internet. People are asking for similar controls in the US. The way we search and access information today on the World Wide Web makes this difficult. Some would claim that it makes it impossible. Regardless, it should not have the government opposing protecting a person's privacy. If the government imposes similar controls in this country, it may exclude government agencies from those controls. It should not even try to do so because from a technology standpoint, access can be controlled. Even better access can be monitored and reported.

More often now, courts view personal information as being owned by the person. Giving an individual a reasonable expectation of privacy based on that view is already happening. These rulings are likely to grow in the coming years. Government is supposed to insure that privacy. Government also has to operate within the law. As a result, the way that federal government treats personal information must change. This change is needed if privacy is to be protected both by and from the government.

Since the 1970s software systems have had to create data security. This became even more important when data could be retrieved on line. Now cloud technology can even split off where the data is stored. This may seem to raise the risks even more. In some ways it does, but it also provides the basis for much greater security. It makes it possible that the owner of the information can now more adequately control who gets to access the data. It is a simple matter of what is called logging to record the access of other authorized entities (such as the access of the tax information). This would be beneficial not only for government information, but for medical records information.

The result would be that the owner has more responsibility for the appropriate access to the information. That way appropriate notifications when the access occurs, both legitimate, and illegitimate provide a major level of defense from intrusion from within an organization.

THE PDS HOUSE AND WINGS

It is easier for most people to think in everyday terms so I used a house as an analogy. That's why I call the PDS an electronic house or your electronic home. It's easier to understand that instead of the folders and subfolders that actually comprise the PDS. The "wings of the house" are to help people to understand that the governmental, health, and identity portions of the house can be split off from each other. And in the government wing, just like a child's bedroom, we can put monitors to see and "hear" what is going on.

And just like you might lock up the tools, people could "lock" doors to the areas of their house that the government should not access.

If it seems like I am implying that government can act like children, you are right. This is true when no one is there to look over their shoulder or they know they can't be caught.

DRIVERS OF THE FNO STRUCTURE

FNO SIZE CONSIDERATION

Federal systems were founded when there was a much smaller population. As the population grew, the agency structure simply attempted to grow in size to support the higher volumes. There has been little done to change the structure to support the much larger number of people. This is true even in the house and senate. There we see that only the members with seniority can actually participate in making decisions. As a result, as the population has grown, each person has had a smaller and smaller voice. The FNO addresses this problem to support more people taking part in government.

The town hall meetings ideals first lead to the concept of a FNO. It has to be relatively small. At the same time, it needed to subdivide people into these groups in an objective manner. Why? This needs to be done in a way that avoids gerrymandering. These goals made the census tract an attractive method of determining the size and population to be served.

There is a point at which the need for services being offered at even a minimal level becomes coupled with effective allocation of resources[12]. It is at that point that a brick and mortar presence is needed.

Being local to the population to be served is also a mandatory pre-requisite for some kinds of services. In that respect the Postal Service the local branches from the 19th and 20th century is a technologically challenged cousin to the FNO.

The difference between the local post office and the FNO was that the post office was designed for the physical movement of mail. Items like passports and selective service notifications were added over time to address some of the same needs that the FNO will now support. The key difference here is that the focus of the FNO is not the physical movement of mail, but rather the access point to government services by the local population.

That local presence has another benefit. It allows technology updates to the overall system to result in improvements in overall service. And it allows that to happen at a reduced cost. All while not being caught in the trap of the old postal service culture.

Another advantage of the FNO, is that most FNO information is either agency data or members PDSs.

----

[12] By resources, is meant the people actually supporting the customer service aspects, as well as the scanners, printers, and access points (e.g., PCs, thin clients, IPOD, IPAD) which are required for gaining some significant cost savings in multiple agencies

This is a big advantage in reducing the physical size of each FNO.

FNO SERVICE DELIVERY

In the private sector, customer touch is a major concern for any portal. The concept of the FNO allows for redefining government customer service. Today when the Internal Revenue **Service** and the Immigration and Naturalization **Service** seem to be anything but services. You may have heard the joke about the most frightening thing a government worker can say. It's "Hi, I'm from the IRS and I'm here to help you".

Changing that view is important if we expect government to actually work better. We have to get to where the idea of an agency actually providing a not laughable. Good service is critical to the success of the FNO model. Moving government services to this new model makes it possible. Federal agency customer service functions can be personalized to the communities. Yet, they can still be standardized. And the entire customer service portal can be managed by the local community. This has the potential to be a huge community benefit. And doing so can fundamentally transform government.

Unlike the US Postal Service, the FNO is intended to have local accountability. The FNO mission is to provide services. Being local allows better "customer touch".

GOVERNANCE OF THE FNO

Without tools, running an FNO service center will be a disaster. Technology needs to be the primary tools through which services are delivered. By taking a private industry concept of a service catalog, standardized services can be "purchased" by each FNO board. This makes a huge difference. Now the tools for running the service center includes the tools for managing the vendors who provide the services at the service center.

Remember, residents of the FNO area determine the board for each FNO. If an FNO service is not up to standards or isn't acceptable, the vendors can be replaced, or if need be the residents can replace the board. This gives the community much more control over what is done thru the FNO. That way the community and the board can maintain their operations.

Using local boards to manage local services can have huge benefits. Giving control to a local board can cut management costs in each agency. Instead it creates one management layer called the FNO board. Even better, each FNO is accountable. Compare that with over 100 agencies each with over 20 layers of management. Then take each agency and multiply it by the number of locations. The number seems very close to the number of FNO sites. But there is a huge difference. Each of these layers effectively has little or no accountability. The FNOs are accountable to their communities.

PLATFORM FOR INPUT

The decision support portion of the FNOs operations is intended to be a suggestion box on steroids. It also provides a 21st century voting model. Using polling and social media software can make identifying and communicating needs much easier. This gives the community an easy way to identify local needs quickly. The FNO can manage local services directly. I believe this delivery model can be less expensive. And this delivery model can respond faster.

The use of polling software can provide secret ballots for recall of boards and magistrates as well. This improves the ability to coordinate, combine and affect local operations. This can improve communications with other local FNOs to form groups to petition the government for their redress of grievances.

IMPROVED RECORD KEEPING

The FNOs provide the opportunity to use video and sound to record decisions. This then allows playback for community members. This by definition provides more transparency than is possible in current governmental structures.

DRIVERS FOR THE FEDERAL ID CARD (FIC)

As the size of the country has grown, so did the need for standardized recordkeeping. As a result in the 1930s, the Social Security Card began to be issued. It let the government keep track of those who were contributing. It also identified those who should receive Social Security Benefits. As the government has grown in the services that it provides, there has been little effort to use that concept in receiving other benefits.

Instead we have separate identifications for separate services. We have VA cars, and food stamp cards. Universities have university IDs etc.

Today it has become obvious that there are many situations where the a federal ID card would be a good idea. The stakes for having a national ID card get even more necessary when you have an FNO and a PDS.

Not only can an ID card be used as an identification, it can be used to control access to personal information. It can be used to receive government benefits. It can be used to provide protections greater than we currently do with our credit cards.

The advantages for the individual far outweigh any privacy issues.

DRIVERS OF THE FLMC

The biggest reason for the FLMC became obvious only after much of this book had been drafted.

Administrative law is a collection of processes which are in the wrong branch of government. The founding fathers clearly had the expectation that the courts would not be part of the executive branch. The judicial branch was intended to protect the states from the power of the executive branch. The idea of protecting the people was only made clear from the Bill of Rights.

Slowly changes occurred in the federal government resulted in what we have today. Administrative law is the law where the courts are part of the executive branch. That is, if there is something called a court. Sometimes, it is called a commission, sometimes there are groups called a board. The common idea for all of these is that they are supposed to determine who is wrong as far as the executive branch is concerned. By definition this is a flaw in the three separate branches of government. Determination of what is the law is the decision of the courts. John Marshall made that clear before the new country was even 20 years old. This flaw of having a court in the executive branch has grown to the point where it is a practice specialty for lawyers.

No one expects the administrative courts to defend their best interests from the government. This is true of the VA hearings on coverage, through the IRS Tax Courts, through the Civil Rights Commission, through the EPA, and on and on. The very existence of these courts within the executive branch at all is in opposition to the intent of the framers of the constitution. There is little doubt that the administrative law functions can possibly be administered in a way that is clearly objective when it is part of the executive branch.

For all of these reasons the FLMC was included in the new design.

But perhaps the biggest reason for the FLMC is that it is in public. The FLMC provides a compelling case for having justice be reached in the public square, rather than in hearings which do not allow for any visibility.

LOCAL RESOLUTION OF PROBLEMS

Many of the conflicts which today have to go to a state court. Worse, they are turned into a federal case. If you can reach justice fairly, it is much better if it can be resolved at the level. Many offenses are called petty in the federal code today. This is not my term. Having those petty offenses be heard in a FLMC makes it quicker to have justice rendered. Further, it doesn't require a massive bureaucracy. Best of all, it can be done for offenses that would otherwise go unpunished. Civil rights cases may make the best example for this, as shown in the stories.

This has several advantages. First, the FLMC can focus on that level of cases which should be at the local level. This would provide for legal enforcement for a large number of cases which aren't brought to the current federal courts because they are too much trouble. Second, by bringing the cases first to the local level, if it can be resolved, it would actually reduce the number of cases brought to the current federal courts. Third, the current administrative courts could have most of the responsibilities moved to the FLMC. This would eliminate the flaw in the current three branches of government.

DRIVERS OF THE FEDERAL INFORMATION SERVICE (FIS)

Over the last 100 years the federal government has continued to grow. This is despite the creation of the Government Accountability Office (GAO). This is despite the creation of the Office of Management and Budget (OMB). It is despite the creation of multiple blue ribbon panels on how to cut government costs. Some of those blue ribbon panels have become permanent additions to the federal government all by themselves. The council of economic advisors is just one example. Even during the grand bargain of the 1990s, the size of the executive branch didn't shrink. And frankly the grand bargain did not even say it was to shrink the government. For the last 40 years we have been vainly attempting to shrink the *rate* of growth of the executive branch. Even with the current sequestration period under Obama, it was again the rate of growth that actually shrunk. In every instance the slowdown was temporary.

Why? The causes are varied. Most of the reasons can be boiled down to a few core drivers.

Agency size is power in the Washington DC social structure

Agency size is based on the dollar spent.

Expenditures for social welfare have risen dramatically.

For decades, the agencies which did not spend almost all their funds were the agencies that had their funding cut. After a year or two of that result, agency heads learn. If an agency head spends all the funds allocated you are seen as being effective. If you are seen as an effective agency, it's easier to get more funds to expend on programs. Unfortunately this is also true of both the so-called watchdog agencies, the GAO and the OMB.

Even if we believe that federal civil service agencies are willing to make significant changes, there is a lot of history that says they won't. It is much more likely that they will find ways to undermine and changes. Or more likely attempt to delay any changes. And worst of all, if you do start to make changes, the agencies themselves may even sabotage the changes. All of that will be to stop any re-engineering effort.

Why?

There have already been efforts to re-engineer within agencies and in most cases they fail. Instead, agencies become more powerful. They become that way first through added legislation increasing the scope and operations of the agency. Often these added jobs of the agency are due to marketing both Congress and the public. You have seen commercials pointing you to federal services. These are paid for by the government. In many cases they are paid for by the agency to demonstrate the criticality of needs. With increased demand, the government has continued an expansion unabated.

Here are at 2 examples.

Efforts to combine agencies when DHS was formed resulting in almost no reduction in any specific agency. Instead the cost of the DHS was added. While everyone agreed there needed to be functional reform of the security agencies, no one seemed to know how. Generally, Congress thought by giving the DHS the purse strings they could bring the other security agencies in line. That has had no success. In fact, it mirrors the success Congress has had with the purse strings of the executive branch. That is, it doesn't stop from adding spending.

The Department of Health and Human Services was created separating out some pieces. The separated pieces went into a new Department of Education. The change was done with good intentions. It was to concentrate on delivery of different services. It did nothing to control the growth of the federal government. After the transition, adding functions continued within each department.

Within HHS there have been multiple additions. These include

State Children's Health Insurance Program.

Vaccines for Children Program.

Nutrition Labeling and Education Act.

Federal Funding for Foster Care and adoption assistance.

Affordable Care Act.

In 1999 HHS launched initiatives to combat bioterrorism. In 2002 the Office of Public Health added emergency preparedness as a result of the anthrax mail scare. Yet in 2014, the Ebola epidemic is now causing some to demand more government. The problem is not more government. The problem is the need for effective government.

In corresponding fashion the Department of Education since 1980 has had the following additional programs added to its stable of support structures.

No Child Left Behind

Family Educational Rights and Privacy Act

IDEA (Individuals with Disabilities Education Act)

Title II and IX expansions

FAFSA (Free Application for Federal Student Aid)

Pre-School Federal Aid

Yet at least for Education, the US rank in the world as far as educational results has continued to decline.

It should be obvious to anyone looking at the problem objectively, we are doing something wrong.

OPTIONS GAO, OMB OR??

The need for a government program to manage starting the FNOs was clear almost from the beginning. Even though the idea of an FNO was fuzzy, it was clear that the FNOs could not be set up like other projects and programs. Something different was needed. Something different had to be done to stop adding to the Babel of government acronym soup. It was then that the idea of a Federal Information Service began to take shape. As the FNO concept became clearer, the need for the Federal Information Service became even more obvious.

One of the more significant questions was "Could an existing government agency actually provide the basis for the programs that would be needed to get the FNO off the ground?" The answer clearly was no.

The next question was where should that agency be? The idea of housing the programs within the executive branch has the obvious advantage of allowing decisions to be quick. However, there are multiple problems with just adding it to the executive branch. First, complaints about the programs be loudest within the executive branch. Second, what will also occur is a lot of turf fighting. This fighting would destroy any chance of success for the FNOs.

Setting up a new agency was a possibility, but a new agency would not have the organizational controls necessary to initiate and orchestrate the changes. We learned that much from the lesson of setting DHS up. Also, a new agency simply will not have the political clout to implement the changes. All of these reasons made a new agency a less than ideal choice.

Putting the program for initiating the FNOs within the Government Accountability Office is seen as the best compromise.

Why? Because the GAO is a creature of the legislative branch as much as it is focused on the executive branch.

WHY A DEPARTMENT NOT JUST A PROJECT OR PROGRAMME

If the FIS were formed as a program, what little clout it has would inevitably be bound into the annual budgeting and organizational control issues that essentially would place the programs in competition with every other program WITHIN the same agency, much less across agencies.

If the FIS comes close to fulfilling its original mandates, it is likely to be hated by other agencies within the federal government. Placing it as part of the GAO is an attempt to protect the new department. This is due to the GAO being in the legislative branch. Putting the functions there is to avoid the budget gamesmanship within the executive and legislative branches. Or at least an attempt to keep the games to a minimum.

CHAPTER 12. NEW FEDERAL AGENCIES

One of the major goals of Gov 2.0 is to improve the federal delivery systems. This effort is huge. To make the needed changes will require both new structures and temporary services. Both the FNO and the FLMC will need to be set up in their entirety. Support functions will need to be first created, then used to support these new structures.

The focal point for all this effort is the Federal Information Service (FIS).

FEDERAL INFORMATION SERVICE

The FIS is a new department within and part of the GAO. Yet, there must be a strong dotted-line relationship to the OMB (Office of Management and Budget). This OMB link is to be sure that there is progress in decentralizing the federal agencies. Only by moving functions to the FNO can Gov 2.0 be called a success.

On a strategic basis, the FIS is responsible for the success of the federal re-engineering program started.

This chapter provides a brief description of the programs, projects and new agencies that will be set up to actually deliver Gov 2.0.

The rest of this chapter may seem like alphabet soup but the soup has meaning. As you read, remember each program and project has a distinct goal and a distinct product. Separating large efforts into projects and programs is a common approach within project management circles.

To most people the difference between project and program is not important. Yet there is a difference between a project and a program. Projects are temporary endeavors undertaken to create a unique product, service or result. Programs are a group of related projects, subprograms, and program activities managed in a coordinated way to obtain benefits not available through managing them individually.[13]

The first this the FIS does is to set up itself as an agency. In addition the FIS is responsible for several distinct programs. These are:

The **Federal Functional Identification Program** (FFIP) will look at all the functional processes of each federal agency. Each process will be identified and standardized, and then categorized. Where the process deals directly with the citizen, it will be redesigned to be performed by the FNO. The remaining processes will be modified to integrate with the new FNO process. The end product of this program will be the processes used in the FNO and re-engineered agency processes for each federal agency which is part of the program.

The **Federal Neighborhood Office** Program **(FNOP)** will establish all the FNOs. This will be done through a set

---

[13] From the Project Management Body of Knowledge manual 5th Edition published by PMI – The Project Management Institute

of projects. The first set of projects is the POC (Proof of Concept) projects which will test the new processes from the FFIP program. Once the POC sites have confirmed the process, the number of FNOs to open will increase during the pilot stage projects. Finally, the bulk of the FNOs will be set up and opened during the main roll out stage projects. In addition the FNOP will create the **FNO Administration Service (FNOAS)**. The FNOAS will provide the administrative oversight of the FNOs after they have been established.

The second set of programs are those which set up the longer term processes for improving service delivery. These are

The Federal Data and Operational Security Administration (FDOSA) project will first set up the FDOSA. The FDOSA sets the standards and rules for the PDS. The FDOSA will also set up the standards and rules for the FIC.

The **Federal Contract Development and Administration (FCDA)** Project publishes contracts for every vendor service. This applies to services to both the FNO and the FLMC. The FCDA has three end products. First is the contract library. Second is the service catalog. The third is the agency itself.

A couple of basic guidelines may help to understand how the parts will work together.

First, whenever an agency has a process that is already done at a local office, it will be moved to the FNOs. This mantra makes one of the purposes of the FIS easier. One roles the FFIP plays is to evaluate other federal agencies processes. When a current process should be performed at a local FNO, the FFIP becomes the responsible group for the redesign. They will decide how it will be done at the FNO and be integrated back to remaining agency processes.

Second, all the federal agencies will need to be re-engineered to integrate with the FNOs. This re-engineering is not as hard as it sounds. As an agency is re-engineered, it will become clear which processes can be performed at the FNOs. They are the processes which have repetitive interactions with multiple users. These will be the focus of the initial re-engineering.

Third, agencies which are already outwardly focused on delivery will be the first to be redesigned. This would include agencies such as the Postal Service and the IRS. This moves the redesign forward more quickly. It also provides the greater impact to making the FNOs an effective operation.

Fourth, as agency processes are reviewed duplicates will be found. Some duplicates may even be found in the same agency. Others will be duplicates of processes done in an agency which has already been re-engineered. In most instances the process will have been moved to the FNO. However, it will be left to the executive branch and congress to decide how this non-customer focused duplicated processes will be performed. They may be done by each agency separately. Or they may be standardized and set up as a service that each agency can use either through the FIS, or by contracting with vendors. The important point is that the duplication is then intentional, not by chance.

Government 2.0 Vision and Architecture
Chapter 12 – New Federal Agencies

Lastly, most of the processes that are moved to the FNOs will not be performed by FNO employees. Instead the processes will be designed as a standard service. That way many different companies can actually perform the process. Once a service is identified and documented, it can be designed to be bought by different vendors. As different vendors come forward to identify which services they offer, FNO boards can judge how well different the different companies perform. It allows the boards to improve services when needed by switching companies. And this can help the local economy as well.

The FNOs and the agency re-engineering described in the next chapter need to be cost effective. As the FNOs open, agency operational expenses must be transferred to the FNOs. Since the services aren't going away, the cost savings would seem to be small. But, since the services are being done by private companies bidding against each other, the savings would be larger than you might expect.

Volume 2 – Design and Implementation Planning has significant details about the FIS. It also has more detail about the other programs and projects. Finally it has some thoughts on making sure that the delivery process is not "rolled back".

The scope and size of the effort to build Gov 2.0 are shown in these program and project summaries.

FFIP PROGRAM

The following projects occur for each agency which is reviewed as part of Government 2.0 The program level provides both the coordination and communication to the Congress. The results of this program determine the scope of the FNOs. The following projects are part of the FFIP Program.

FUNCTION IDENTIFICATION

This project identifies each process within the selected Federal Agency. For each process, the project will recommend either

- The process be kept as part of the agency

- The process be moved to the FNO.

- No change is necessary for the process.

These results will be presented to Congress to confirm or modify. For the agency changes approved by Congress the following projects will be undertaken

FUNCTIONAL REDEFINITION

This project updates the remaining agency functions. This is to assure that agency operations are effective.

PROCESS DEFINITION

This project updates the process manuals and service contract requests for the approved functions for the FNOs. These updates are sent to the FNOAS and the FCDAS to complete setting up the new processes.

FNO PROGRAM

This program manages all the projects required to standup the new Federal Neighborhood Offices and the overarching structure.

These include project such as:

FNO POLICIES, PROCEDURES AND STANDARDS PROJECT

This project is responsible for

- o Selection of PDS and FIC vendors for the POC
- o Constructing the first manuals for the POC
- o Initial version of Standards for
  - ▪ PDS storage vendors,
- o Initial standards for the FIC
- o All service contracts for POC vendors
- o All service contract templates for vendors for the pilot phase

FNO PROOF OF CONCEPT

This project is responsible for starting a minimum of 15 Federal Neighborhood Offices (FNO) s. These FNOs will represent a wide range of geographic and resident characteristics. The objective is to have as much diversity as possible to prove the value of the FNO.

FNO PILOT PROJECT

The FNO Pilot project is responsible to take the lessons learned from the FNO POC project and to roll out to about 700 FNO sites nationwide. In addition this project is responsible to determine the scalability and speed of the full rollout of the remaining 69,000 sites.

FNO FULL ROLLOUT

The FNO Full Rollout project has the responsibility to roll out to the remaining 69,000 sites at a realistic roll out speed. It is expected that this will be a multi-year project.

FNO TRANSITION PROJECT

The FNO Transition Project has two objectives. The first is to set up the Federal Neighborhood Office Administration Service (FNOAS). The second task is to shut down the previous FNO Projects. While doing the second task they will be transferring responsibilities to the FNOAS.

FNO ADMINISTRATION SERVICE (FNOAS)

Like the FIS, the FNOAS would be a new federal agency. Initially the FNOAS will be part of the FIS. Once the re-engineering efforts are completed, the service should be transitioned to the executive branch. In the executive branch it could function either as a separate agency, or as a service within the FIS. The FNOAS will be responsible for

- Maintaining the FNO operations by
  - Maintaining standards of operations for the FNO.
  - Maintaining procedures to be used by GAA vendors to the FNO offices.
  - Adding functions to the FNO Offices as needed.

FEDERAL DATA AND OPERATIONAL SECURITY ADMINISTRATION (FDOSA)

FDOSA will be responsible for the protection of individual's privacy and electronic identity. FDOSA will be in charge of setting the data security standards for the FIC. FDOSA will also set the access standards for the PDS. To do this will require working with other federal agencies. Here are some examples.

FIC STANDARDS

FDOSA will work with the Social Security Administration (SSA) to replace the Social Security Card. FDOSA will set the standards, features and format of the FIC card. Every agency that uses an ID card will be impacted by FDOSA. This is why having the FNOs produce the ID card is important.

FDOSA also approves the FIC GAA vendors.

PDS STANDARDS

FDOSA sets the rules on how the government can access and utilize a PDS. This includes the rules on notifications to the person who owns the PDS.

To do this, the government needs to be able to know where you keep your information. Storage vendors need to be given the format of the information that will be requested and returned. This is also true for the medical records data.

Vendors who provide PDSs need to know the rules on how to check an individual ID. Your FNO must give you with that secure identifier. And the agency must tell the vendor the rules on how to use the FIC.

Also, PDS vendors by law are required to notify you of **all** accesses to your information.

One comment about standards is important. Setting standards does not mean making it so that only one vendor can meet the standard. This is common in government contracts today. It is a major reason why government services cost so much today.

Another concern should be about how many PDS vendors are needed. A single provider of the US PDS capability is a problem. One vendor may gain the public trust, but that trust must be earned. With multiple vendors, those who do not maintain effective security can lose customers. The standards for PDSs and the contracts for PDSs must support having multiple PDS vendors.

In effect FDOSA is in charge of the security and access standards and methods. Even better they do this while having no access to the data itself.

Further FDOSA will be also be responsible for establishing and maintaining the standards under which information about individuals in executive branch agencies can be accessed without violating the individual's rights of privacy. Since the legal methods of access to an individual's PDS are managed by FDOSA, they are implicitly also responsible for at least recommending what constitutes a crime in violating the privacy of an individual, along with what are appropriate accesses.

While most of the changes identified as New Federal Structures deals with new Federal Executive or Legislative Departments, there is a need for clear privacy enforcement legislation regarding the Personal Data Stores.
Chapter 15 contains further information on the outlines of what the federal criminal code needs regarding your information and the federal government. Because of the relationship between security standards and appropriate access in effect FDOSA becomes heavily involved with the setting of appropriate standards for data access.

FIS CONTRACT DEVELOPMENT AND
ADMINISTRATION SERVICE (FCDAS)

There really are only a few types of contracts. Most government contracts are awarded on the basis that a single award is made to a single vendor. This leads to heavy negotiation on the Terms and Conditions. Despite the length of the negotiations, they still end up looking very much the same. The government can read the contract as saying they will get something specific. The vendor will read the contract as saying they will give something specific. The contract will say that both are correct. The contracts also include enough exceptions, that effectively both the government and the vendor have to budget for attorneys when the contract comes to an end. Why? Because not only does the government say what they expect the contract to do, they also tell the vendor how to do it. This results in the government having a second and even a third vendor who have their own contracts. Those secondary contracts describe how these added vendors will oversee the first vendor. And even then, we have government workers who have titles like Contracts Manager, who then are in charge of checking the first three vendor contracts. With this as the "normal" way of contracting, you can see how the lawyers end up with a great income from government contract disputes. As a result the contracts all contain entire sections dealing with exceptions and disputes. In simple terms, the contracts are filled with weasel words. Weasel words are the pieces of a contract that say, "It's not our fault, it's the other guys fault".

But before you even get to where you can argue about what is being developed there is yet another hurdle.

Vendor protests are so common that larger companies actually assume any award they get will be protested. What is a protest? When a company claims that the award process is unfair, they file a protest. There are entire departments in some agencies that deal only with protests. And the reason protests are filed, is that sometimes they work. But most of the time, the winning company cuts a piece of the work out in a way that the other company becomes a subcontractor. Basically, they want a "taste" of the government pork.

Obviously, this is not a good way to get goods and services. It does nothing to maximize the satisfaction with either the goods or the service. It certainly doesn't increase competition. And it definitely does not cause services to be delivered with quality.

Instead of the contracting version of the pork barrel polka, there is another way. The easiest way is to describe what the service delivery needs to be to be paid. Nothing in the contract about oversight, management, methodology, or oversight. The contract should say in a direct manner what we expect the vendor to do. We should accept what the vendor will charge for the service, and how long we are setting the contract length. But what we should not do, is only contract with one vendor. We should contract with as many vendors as possible. Only then can we be that entrepreneurship is occurring.

Both the overall effort and the FNO rollout will take advantage of current contract forms. One of the more common and easiest to change is called IDIQ. It stands for Indefinite Delivery Indefinite Quantity. You could legitimately create IDIQ agreements with as many vendors as would wish to provide the service. I do not think these contracting methods have ever been used to build competition. Contracts should pay vendors for quality services rendered. Being able to select from a number of vendors will foster competition.

While a large number of contracts will in the end be signed, the very fact that there are so many duplicative services provided across 70,000 Federal Neighborhood Offices means that standardized contracts are mandatory.

What's more, procedures and requirements to be met for the delivery of these services must be defined in sufficient detail that the same service provided by different vendors at different locations has the chance to be the same high levels of accuracy, efficiency and effectiveness.

While the focus seems to be on the FNOs and FLMCs just as much change is required within each agency. Each agency need to be changed to support privacy requirements. They also must change to make services more effective. Lastly, they must change to support decentralization. This provides ample chance for effective re-engineering at the agency level as well.

For all of these reasons, the initial FFIP project was the initial project for Government 2.0.

It is the FFIP that will determine what level of description is necessary for a service to be developed and sold by vendors to the FNOs.

It will do so by performing the following:

The FFIP project will initially create contracts to support the re-engineering of the agency operations through a standardized contract for each agency.

1. Agency Functional Identification and Allocation Contracts.

The results of that initial set of contracts will be sufficient to drive standardized contracts for

2. Agency Functional Specification Contracts

3. Agency Re-engineered Process Contracts

4. Agency Operations Execution Contracts

Contracts to create FNOs FLMCs and to support the operations of these new entities will also be needed for

5. Service Definition Contracts

6. Service Development Contracts

7. Service Operations Contracts

The contract structures will be similar for each agency and for each Federal Neighborhood Office opening.

CHAPTER 13. AGENCY CHANGES

This chapter is only intended to show what can be done to make the federal agencies work better. This chapter shows what kinds of changes can make an agency more customer-centric. This chapter also describes how to make agencies more efficient. By moving some functions to the FNOs, operations become more manageable for the agencies. The agencies themselves won't end up looking exactly like what is described here. But by applying changes in the way described by the FFIP we can expect to make changes along these lines.

Unless we actually look at changing the way we deliver services, no changes will occur at the agencies. It is human nature to keep change at a level where it is comfortable. While less obvious, it is very uncomfortable to introduce change when it may cause you to lose your job. This is true whether the change is in business or government. And yet, we have to change if we are to get to the point where we can again manage our own government.

There is a positive result of changing the local arms of the federal government. By implementing the FNOs, people can expect to be able to control their own operations. As a result, they should be more willing to participate. They will also be able to see the result of that effort. This in turn allows governmental services to concentrate on service. Today unfortunately, most federal agencies have to focus on enforcement. This won't have big impacts on some federal agencies, like say the National Park Service. For others like the IRS or the Postal Service this can result in enormous changes in attitude and process.

For example, the IRS clearly has a process and a culture which insures that the public is going to be an adversary. In some respects the same is true with Social Security. Changing the process from being the "bad guys" to being a service will help to change the views. By moving the services from a few locations all run by DC to the local neighborhood will help to change the attitudes even more. Finally having the service run by the local community will cause the change to be permanent. Just as important, all of these changes will change the views that the government workers have about people.

REDESIGNED US POSTAL SERVICE

Today, the USPS makes every attempt it can to keep the costs of mail as low as possible. Yet, at the same time, it cannot close post offices because of public pressure. It cannot move mail to email because that technology is viewed as being the cause of the USPS's problems. Email is actually the solution to most of the USPS problems, along with completely changing its process.

Because everyone has a PDS and a public email address email should be even easier than it is now. In fact, most mail would never even need to be printed. However, there are times where either the sender or the receiver still wants or needs physical mail. For these cases, the postal service will still provide carrier pickup, but it will be on a lighter schedule. With the amount of mail already lower, and Gov 2.0 making it even easier to email, there does not need to be a six-day delivery schedule. Making it into a three-day delivery schedule would certainly reduce the costs.

Rates for electronic mail delivery will be much lower than mail is today.

To further cut costs, once the local FNO is running, mail delivery can be contracted out. Local companies can provide the pickup and delivery services. FedEx, UPS and the postal service itself will be able to bid for the contracts. In more populated areas, small businesses can compete as well.

Local PO Boxes will no longer be part of separate USPS facilities instead will be part of the FNO.

Bulk mail business operations can offer targeted marketing by hour instead of by week. Using the new emails they can target zip codes with a timing that now can't be done. Today, they must send mail using a window for delivery of a day or even a week. With email immediacy, targeted campaigns can be kicked off for a noon start just as an example.

REDESIGNED INTERNAL REVENUE SERVICE

In the stories chapter it is clear that the changes for the IRS are immense. In fact, the changes completely change the way a tax return is completed, reviewed and accepted by the IRS. The current structure is sent up based on the probability that the returns are largely both accurate and honest. Those which are not accurate are presumed to be dishonest.[14]. The new structure being defined does fundamentally change that approach.

Most taxpayers are individuals. For them, the completion of an accurate return becomes the responsibility of a Government Authorized Agent (GAA) vendor like TurboTax or H&R Block. These companies will need to apply and receive GAA status. These vendors become agents of the individual. They are now responsible for making sure the return is accurate. They become responsible for insuring that the individual complies with the law. Any audit of the return will be a review of the GAA not the individual taxpayer.

Even better, the PDS will now hold the individuals financial data. This data which is needed for the tax returns will be stored where the GAA can access it. The government can also access it. And with the way the PDS is built, the accesses can be monitored to see who is accessing it. This is a much greater privacy protection than what we have today.

While not referenced in these stories, individuals who cannot afford to pay for their own GAA vendor, or who elect not to select one, will have a GAA IRS vendor assigned based on the selection of the board of the FNO.

---

[14] Once when I had made a mistake and was contacted by the IRS, I spent just as long explaining how I made the mistake as it took to actually correct the problems

There are other advantages to the IRS changes. Using GAAs allows for tax payments and returns to be done more rapidly. And it will reduce the collection of late payments. Why? Because the vendors will now become more responsible in cutting the cost of their business. Running the process longer costs more.

Because the structure is intended to be voluntary in its use, the ability to actually calculate and file your own return without any vendor would still be available, BUT it is unlikely that this would be the case for most people. For those who insist on filing their own paper return, the GAA vendors will be able to bid on handling those returns as well.

REDESIGNED SOCIAL SECURITY ADMINISTRATION

The SSA, and IRS and USPS were among the first government functions to be automated. All three agencies were automated back in the 1950s thru 1970s. These systems are old. Their systems show all the problems described about old systems.

The SSA is one of several "faces" of the government. The SSA has over 1200 offices nationwide. It also includes offices in United States Embassies across the world[15]. It has almost 60,000 employees, with headquarters in Baltimore.

The SSA has a Board of Trustees. In theory the board manages the entire fund. In reality, the board is simply a method by which the operations of the SSA are stamped and approved. Why? Five of the seven members of the board are already in executive positions within the Federal Government. The Board must rely on permanent staff to make the decisions which in effect the board automatically approved. The two individuals who are not already in the government must not be in the same political party. However you look at the board makeup, it is clear that these two positions are political plum positions. While some management of the SSA fund would be useful if the fund actually had any meaning, it really doesn't. The only investment the SSA

---

[15] The numbers and references described in this section come from the Social Security Website as of October 2014.

makes is into the US Treasury. The complexity is
mostly to make it seem like the SSA is independent.
The reality is that the government functions now
depend on the SSA.

When originally founded the SSA was organized around
a concept of a "Fund". SSA is now responsible for two
separate funds.

Social Security Trust Fund

Medicare Trust Fund

The SSA in the broadest sense really only has a few
functions. For the Social Security Trust Fund, the basic
functions are to maintain a financial Fund. The SSA is
also supposed to receive payments into the fund. They
are also supposed to manage payments from the fund.
Lastly, they are supposed to manage the ongoing
investments of the fund.

To do this, the SSA has the following processes

- The SSA issues Social Security Cards which
  point to individual accounts.

- The SSA confirms social security numbers for
  businesses.

- The SSA keeps the contribution history of the
  individual.

- The SSA confirms what benefits can be paid.

- The SSA pays the benefits.

These last five items are all being completely upgraded with Gov 2.0

The 1200 US offices of the SSA would be merged into the over 60,000 FNOs. This includes applying for cards and accounts. It also includes applications to receive benefits.

The processes to provide confirmation to employers becomes part of the PDS. The storage of the contribution history also becomes part of the PDS.

The Administrative Law functions of the SSA are moved to the FLMCs. To get an idea of the volume of cases, one statistic I saw had over 600,000 cases per year.

VETERANS ADMINISTRATION REFORM AND AUTOMATION IMPROVEMENTS

While some minor aspects of the VA operate effectively, even minor improvements can have big impacts. I've listed two areas impacted by Gov 2.0 but there are likely to be more.

Speeding up the creation of the Electronic Medical Records (EMR) will benefit all veterans. A complete EMR will reduce delays in receiving treatment. Paper files need to be moved, and can be just plain lost. EMRs can be backed up and are immediately available.

The benefit to a veteran of having a local office like the FNO cannot be overstated. Today the way the VA routes and schedules the veteran for treatment are awful. The need for services is obviously greater than the system is actually equipped to handle. The FNO can redirect delayed patients into the local health systems if it becomes necessary. This has to provide a benefit to the veteran.

Right now the delivery bottlenecks within the VA limit the costs of services. There is a maximum service cost based on the number of people who can provide the service. Allowing other doctors to help will not drive the per service cost higher, but because a more veterans are receiving timely services, the cost will rise. In this specific instance, that is a good thing. Right now we don't have good costs because vet's have to wait far too long.

Additionally whether the care is for a condition related, or unrelated to the veteran's service history, local physicians and hospitals and care facilities could be used to reduce the level of dysfunction within the VA.

When the VA is delinquent the FNO advocate can be a tremendous help to the veteran. Local veterans will have the FNO advocate working on their behalf. FNO advocates won't have a conflict of interest that affects VA personnel. In fact, it may help VA personnel to reduce the bureaucracy in the VA itself.

FEDERAL WELFARE PROGRAM REFORM SERVICES

The ability to target local needs and priorities cannot be overemphasized. The FNO can provide that ability. One size does not fit all, and local FNOs can be much more effective at targeting needs.

In today's centralized view, all changes from the federal government need to come from the Congress or the

Executive branch. This tends to make programs be defined in broad strokes which forces spending higher. A portion of the funding is spent on insuring that ONLY people meeting the broad stroke qualifications receive the service. And of that portion, the same data about the person is gathered for each service. The PDS can reduce that data gathering significantly.

What's more, services are duplicated across agencies, depending on who is to be receiving the service. Today there are special programs for the American Indians, blacks, and service veterans. And some portions of these programs are to deliver the same service. By making service delivery separate, it will reduce this duplication. This in itself will reduce costs. This will reduce the amount of data that needs to be gathered.

Finally because the program is centralized, the cost of administration tends to be higher. This reduces the amount available to deliver the service.

FEDERAL ELECTION COMMISSION AUTOMATION IMPROVEMENTS

Current campaign reporting is both inefficient and ineffective. It does not provide useful information to the people it was supposed to inform. It certainly does not do it on a timely basis. It seems as though the Federal Election Commission (FEC) is meeting only the letter of the legislation. Since the FEC was intended to allow people to see who is contributing to campaigns, the monthly reporting does not seem nearly often enough. As a result. The FEC doesn't meet any of the objectives that the Congress formed the commission to meet.

Upgrades to the processing are easy if you assume that the information should be both easy to access and easy to analyze. While it is technically easy to access, it is almost impossible to analyze. Why? Because it is built off the forms the FEC produced when it first started. There is little standardization of names and data. Further, the website itself says that some forms of analysis are an improper use of the information. This appears to be based on administrative decisions. Some will claim the rules are submitted for review by congress. I have not been able to find where the limitations about using the data were ever actually submitted. Even if they were, limiting the use of information itself seems to be an infringement of individual rights.

Applying the concepts of Gov 2.0 to the Federal Election Commission is obvious. The only reason that I can see to make things difficult for the citizen to access and analyze is that the objective is NOT to provide timely information.

Privatizing the functions of the Federal Election Commission can identify several kinds of GAAs. These are based on the data sets currently available to the end user in the current PDF form, but should be redefined into a format that allows both browsing (as the PDF currently does) but also data structures more capable of supporting the needs of data analysis vendors.

Vendors should be able to become certified for one or more of the following FEC reporting requirements;

- Candidate FEC Required Filing Services

- PAC FEC Required Filing Services
- Political Party FEC Required Filing Services

Each vendor for supporting both candidates and PACs should provide daily-automated updates to the Federal Election Commission for all funds received. The FEC should then make this information available on a next day basis. This in turns allows the data analysis services access to current data, not data that is already old before it reaches the public's ability to access it.

CHAPTER 14. SUPPORTING COMPONENTS

US FEDERAL ID CARD

The US Federal Identification Card (FIC) is a simple concept. It will look like a Driver's license. It will have special security features. Some of these features were mandated after 9/11. And yet some of those features were never completed implemented.

Because of the various types of information that can be carried on the card. FIC cards will need to be modifiable. Changes to the FIC card contents will be one of the services the FNO provides.

The government has a term for the information which uniquely identifies a person. It is called Personal Identifying Information or PII for short. Some PII info will be visible on the card, some will be carried within the card. That second set of info can be read only by special card readers. Each time your card is swiped, a logging record in your PDS would be created in the Government Wing. This logging is done to protect your info from unauthorized access or use. Any updates to the card also are logged. A public key would display which would allow most people to look up your identity assuming you hadn't opted out of that capability.

Just like a credit card, there will be a magnetic strip. The strip carries enough information to identify the card owner. The card will also have an added PIN key known only to the cardholder. This is in addition to the

PIN that most bankcards carry. At the cardholders (and banks discretion), the FIC may be used as a credit or debit card.

USES OF THE FIC

FEDERAL USES OF THE ID CARD

- The FIC would be the primary federal ID card.
- As the means by which you can control the ways those federal agencies can access your government information.
- As a means to access your US PDS (Personal Data Store) from any Personal Computer equipped with an appropriate card reader.
- The FIC could be used in an emergency by health care professionals with proper clearance to access the Medical Record on the persons PDS by qualified health providers.
- Access to the Government Federal Agency information in the Individuals PDS Government wing, current eligibility for such things as VA benefits, Medicare, etc. would be accessible from that agencies unique identifier. [16]

PUBLIC FUNDS DEBIT CAPABILITY

For individuals receiving benefits such as SNAP (food stamps) the card can be used as a restricted debit card

---

16 For most purposes these Unique IDs will not be directly accessed by the cardholder, but will allow the Personal Data Store Government command center to display the current eligibility when requested by the owner.

in addition but separate from the overall general Debit card.

OPTIONAL STATE USAGES OF THE FIC

States will have the option to allow the use of the Federal ID Card for many different services including the following.

- o   Income Tax ID.
- o   Access to unemployment benefits.
- o   Access to welfare benefits.
- o   As a State Drivers' ID
- o   Voter ID
- o   Voter History.[17]

OTHER USES

- When authorized as a debit card, a FIC can be used to receive funds from any federal agency.
- If the states participate, it could be used by states in the same way
- Banks would be able to use the card just like a bank debit card today.

The FNO could use the FIC card to control access to the local FNO site, as well as for documenting the FNO voting activity.

---

17 This is NOT a way of determining whom you voted, just a way to identify that you did in fact vote on a particular date in a particular jurisdiction.

THE PERSONAL DATA STORE NETWORK (PDSN)

The Personal Data Store Network (PDSN) is a federal network. It serves a unique purpose which is to provide an access path to each person's PDS. To do this the PDSN gets information from each vendor who maintains the PDS for the individual. As individuals move between PDS vendors, the PDSN would be updated to contain the new access path, and the old path would be dropped after the move has been completed.

PDSN FEATURES

Most search engines like Google would be modified to support searching for a person on the PDSN. But the search would only return information on the person's "front porch".

GAAs can use the PDSN to gain approved access the individual's information. One significant aspect of the rules about the PDS is that any GAA software NOT keep any PDSN data. The single exception to this is the agency Individual ID. That ID is itself an index within the PDSN.

PDSN SUPPORT FOR INDIVIDUAL PRIVACY

Each time an individual's information is requested, the PDSN will log the access request. That information will be logged both by the agency and within the individual PDS. The biggest use of the PDSN from the individual's standpoint is the ability to demand on request a listing of the PDS accesses by the government. This can be compared to the logging retained in the individual's PDS as an audit measure in the event that there is a concern about privacy.

VENDOR SERVICES ONLINE CATALOG

Multiple vendors will become certified as GAAs. As the number of GAAs grows, there will be a greater need for an online catalog. The catalog will list vendors who can be used by the FNO boards, as well as by GAAs for subcontractors.

Among the primary features of the catalog would be the following:

CATALOG SEARCH VARIATIONS

When a service is added, the service area that the vendor is in is also recorded. As a result, FNOs looking will be able to see who offers a service locally.

(I) ACCESS BY SERVICE

Each Service which can be separately contracted for can be searched by Service, by Vendor, or in combination to get to the appropriate vendors.

(II) ACCESS BY CONTRACT TEMPLATE SERVICES

Some vendors may actually provide services according to different templates. One template may be based on the number of people in the FNO, the next may be a fixed price template. Filtering the list by these types of contracts will help the FNOs

OTHER ACCESSIBLE ITEMS WITHIN THE SERVICE CATALOG

- GAA Service Contracting Templates
- Service Template FNO Voting questions
- Vendor Service Satisfaction / Issue History

OPTIONAL COMPONENTS

In addition to the FIC and the PDSN there are several features which could be added. These optional components are to demonstrate how the new features of Gov 2.0 can grow and extend.

THE FEDERAL ELECTRONIC VOTING SYSTEM (FEVS)

The Federal Electronic Voting System (FEVS) is a standardized voting system. It is authorized by Congress to be made available to the States. Individual states would approve its use. Where states approve the use, the state can interface to the PDS just like any other PDS vendor. There, the state can confirm whether an individual has voted in an election. The state can also update the information to show the person has voted. This information would be in the government "wing" of the PDS. That particular "room" in the government wing has two lists one of which has the following data.

Jurisdiction where the individual has voted (Usually the state county precinct).

The date that the individual voted.

The date of the election.

For states that use of the FEVS, this information will be checked when a person votes. If they have not yet voted, when their vote is completed the information will be updated. If the information indicates the person has already voted, the state would decide the correct action. This could include, rejecting the vote or marking the vote as provisional. If there is no record already recorded for that election date, the list will be updated with that information.

The second list in that room will be the FNO local voting history which will have the same information separately from the state list.

FEDERAL ELECTRONIC STUDY HALL

The following is an example of how the neighborhood concept can be used to provide smaller targeted federal and state programs.

The concept that the federal government allows for deductions in a wide variety of areas is nothing new. Today however, we have no way to use deductions on a neighborhood level. The FNO can provide that method.

A deduction from taxes for parents or grandparents who actively support students studying is an example of what could be done once the FNOs and PDSs are fully in place. It would require legislation that would allow for a specific deduction amount. The legislation could then target individual neighborhoods by having;

- Local Schools and State Laws agreeing to participate in the Federal Study Hall
- Student tutorials or study aids get created within a document library either
    - By the teacher specific to the class and/or student
    - By the district specific to the grade level and subject
    - By the state specific to the grade level and subject

Using that structure, students and their study mentor (usually parents but could be grandparents, guardians, or even paid tutors could retrieve study docs from the library. The documents could then be used by the students by the mentor.

- Saving of the documents in a completed fashion to the student's government PDS.

From that parents could claim a deduction. The deduction could be based on a number of different things. For example, the deduction could be based on the number of documents which are completed. Or the number of documents that the student successfully completed. Or the hours that the documents are expected to take. Each of these measures becomes practical when the information is stored by the individual.

To repeat, the above is more an example of what could be done not what must be done.

INDIVIDUAL CONVICTION HISTORY

Many other things become possible when you think in terms of both services and government. One is that the Federal Government could use of the Government PDS to retain the person's conviction history. Having a combined copy of the individual's conviction history makes other services easier for both the person and the government.

GETTING RECORDS CLEARED

Getting records cleared is important if people are to be re-enter the community. This makes it easier to both request and receive restoring their franchise.

ELIGIBILITY FOR LOCAL OFFICE

Having a local copy an individual can effectively demonstrate their qualifications for FNO office, local and state offices without questions lingering.

COMBATTING IDENTIFY THEFT

While most people think of identity theft as a means for getting access to your bank and credit card accounts, the fact is that especially for minor crimes, being informed when a fake "you" has been arrested because you were being impersonated, will actually assist in reducing identity theft as well.

GOVERNMENT 2.0
THE REQUIREMENTS

CHAPTER 15. CRITICAL REQUIREMENTS

The following sections are frankly the most important portion of the book. Why? Because the requirements are the most important thing to know when re-engineering a system. This is true especially when the objective is re-engineering the government. Normally when you look at a "how to" book, you expect to see the reasons for a book be the first chapter or at least the first paragraphs.

So why is this almost at the end of the book? Because if we started off by saying let's change the government, you probably would have put the book down. But, since by now it's likely that you actually at least browsed the first portion of the book, you are likely to want to read this portion of the book as well. While it is the critical ingredient, I held it back because if you hit the goals too soon most people would stop reading.

OVERARCHING REQUIREMENTS (OR GOALS)

Goals don't necessarily have to change, but if there is a need to change goals, it should be done before a new system is designed.

We don't really have to look hard to find the goals and requirements. They are in the founding documents.

The goals were beautifully described right in the preamble to the Constitution. The government is needed to:

Form a more perfect union,

Establish justice,

Insure domestic tranquility,

Provide for the common defense,

Promote the general welfare,

Secure the blessings of liberty to ourselves and our posterity.

Even though the delivery systems needs to be upgraded, we don't need to actually change these goals.

But while the goals don't need to be changed, there is some benefit to making them clear in the 21st century. Why? Because the way we use words today is different now from what they meant in 1791. Also, we've changed the way the federal, state, and the individual relate to each other. The US Constitution was initially designed to set the rules for the relationship between the federal and the state governments. This was done in addition to describing the structure of the federal government. It was NOT designed to set the relationship between the government and the individual. That's why the people demanded the Bill of Rights before the Constitution was even signed. For most people the Bill of Rights and the Constitution represents a single document. It's the reason most children are taught that the Bill of Rights is a founding document.

This is also why the Constitution and the Bill of Rights ARE the initial set of requirements for the government.

But the meanings of some of the words have changed just a bit from when they were first written.

Historically, the single biggest change in our society was the agonizingly slow transition to even attempting to apply laws to all people equally. We still have work to do to make this happen.

The relationship between the individual, the government and the states is not currently *explicitly* defined in the Constitution. The original document unfortunately also included some things very much at odds with individual liberty such as slavery.

Today as a society, most people would agree that ***government at all levels must insure protection of the rights of all individuals without regards to who they are, who they know, how they look, what they think, and what they say, or how much money and power they have.***

This has huge implications because that is not the way it's been built over the last 225 years. It would be much better to clarify the state and federal responsibilities for protection of the rights of the people, as well as to clarify the actual rights being protected.

See if you agree with the following.

A person being actively denied their rights is a crime by a person or persons against other person or persons. In every single case, it is a crime against people by people.

A person should have the right to bring charges against another person for abridging their rights. While technically people have that right, the cost of doing so is outrageous. As a result, people only attempt to protect their rights when there is someone with "deep pockets" to pay the damages.

Here's an example from the past 20 years. Denny's restaurant chain was sued for discrimination in its service. The suit was not directly against all of the individuals who refused to offer service. The suit was filed against the entire restaurant chain. Now was the injury done only by the restaurant chain, or was the person who refused to serve the patron the one who should have been sued? If you were the person who was told that they would not be served, would you be angry at the chain, or the person who actually said you can't dine here. Perhaps you would be angry with both, but I can guarantee you will be angry with the server.

When a police officer detains a person without probable cause is that not discrimination? Didn't that policeman violate the detained person's rights? Of course they did. But does that mean the police cannot detain a person because of objective criteria that when applied indicate the person should be detained? Of course the policeman should, because frankly that is a part of doing their job.

We need to start dealing directly with the issues like discrimination in ways that help to build a better society, rather than to build more gaps between our communities.

By their very nature racial prejudice and discrimination have had a terrifying impact on the way we think about each other. The worst aspect of that thinking is that discrimination it still exists. Even though we've made progress, in recent years, some people claim that we've actually lost ground. They blame this on continuing things like affirmative action programs. They claim that we've actually increased the separation between the black and white communities. There is some evidence to support this. When something like that is observed it is a significant design consideration.

OTHER CAVEATS

You will see in other places in the book that I place decisions on the state level as being optional. That's because this book is about the federal government. Like the federal government, state changes are for individual states to make. The Constitution was not intended to drive what the states must do. The basic idea is that the powers not reserved to the federal government belong to the state or the people. Because of that relationship in the Constitution, this book mirrors that decision.

Also, even though it is also a design concern, let's realize that some current hot issues will also at least need to be argued on a common ground if any change is to occur at all.

Specifically this include race, religion, social relations, along with privacy and belief.

CRITICAL REQUIREMENTS (GOAL) CHANGES SUMMARY

So what about the need to change the goals for the Constitution regarding the individual? I would suggest getting the goals correctly identified is the biggest single need for Gov 2.0 to get right.

Here's a **possible** set of changes for the goals with the additions/changes in red.

Form a more perfect union,

Establish justice *for all citizens equally*

Insure domestic tranquility,

Provide for the common defense *and protection of all the citizens*,

Promote the general welfare *of all citizens*,

Secure the blessings of liberty to ourselves and our posterity *by insuring the protection of the natural rights of action, belief, association, life, equal treatment before the law, property, and privacy for all individuals.*

While these are four small changes at least as far as rights of the individual, the implications are enormous.

GOVERNMENT ROLE AS ARBITER OF RIGHTS

Government's roles include deciding when the public good outweighs an individual's rights. Making that decision at the proper level of government is also a matter of judgment. In fact, that decision is at the core of many public debates (good and bad). The balancing of these rights between and among people is a legitimate role of the government, so long as it is a balance, not an elimination of one right in deference to another.

RIGHTS HIERARCHY AS GUIDING DESIGN PRINCIPLES

Up until this point, we've discussed the new components as though the design of the government hasn't changed. But in fact it has changed a lot since 1791.

In fact, changes to the government structure have continued to occur almost without interruption since the beginning. Sometimes the changes were made through legislation, sometimes by court decision, or sometimes by executive order. Most of these changes are to one group of people in favor or over another group of people. This even applies to slavery. Slavery was an abomination. But we need to realize that the changes to eliminate slavery did alter the balance between two groups. It was a balance that needed to change. But nevertheless it was a change. To most groups who "lost" because of the change, the change was perceived as unfair. They saw the change as illegitimate or even unconstitutional. The fact is, sometimes these changes are to make things fair, like abolishing slavery. Sometimes, the change is just as unfair as claimed, like the Dredd Scott decision, or the Japanese internment.

You may say, that these weren't changes. And from one point of view the structure didn't change much. But the fact is, the changes to the structure occurred with each minor change. It's only the major changes that most people notice.

This set of disagreements between various groups is important from a design standpoint in only a few respects. These include:

- Was the change because the government was responding to a need? Or was it to fix a problem with the operation of the system?

- Was the change an attempt to make government alter the behavior of one group at the expense of another?

- Did the changes have unforeseen negative consequences? If it did, were the consequences addressed? Or is the system still affected by the side effects of the change?

- Is there a simpler way of actually making the system function more efficiently? Is there a way to make the changes while still supporting the critical and overarching requirements? Is there a way to reduce the negative side effects?

Changes to address identified needs are spread through all 225 years of our history. Most actually did improve the system. We notice the important ones. For example John Marshall clarifying the role of the judiciary branch is still taught in school as the basis for the role the federal courts have.

In a way you can consider laws as being detail requirements. Some detail requirements (laws) were even retained from English common law. Most of these detail requirements were good, but a few have had negative consequences. A redesign should be aware of these deficiencies, at the least to minimize continued impacts.

To arrive at one way of seeing rights as requirements is worth the effort. It shows a presumed hierarchy or rights. Some of the hierarchy is consistent with other writers' views, some are a result of seeing how they have been designed into our government, and how they can be delivered more effectively.

CHAPTER 16.   THE HIERARCHY OF RIGHTS

From a systems architecture standpoint, clear definition of terms is critical. A well-designed system needs this clarity. It's unlikely that a system will be either effective or efficient without clear terms. It almost certainly will not be maintainable. And a system cannot be extended without have clear terms. So in that sense having a clean definition of what is meant by "a right" is extremely important to the overall architecture and design.

It appears that there are several different kinds of rights. Some rights are called Natural. Other rights are call Constitutional. Still others are called legislated and adjudicated. Each of these names a kind of right in terms of its source.

Why do we look to where the source of rights is? Because sometimes, and especially in the case of the U.S Constitution, the source of the right is as important as what the specific right is.

NATURAL RIGHTS AND ENTITLEMENTS

So what is meant by natural rights? You can Google it and come up with a wide range of definitions. Most of these definitions are given as examples. Natural rights however, generally don't include rights that are a result of the creation, management or operation of a government. These rights were according to the way the US government was founded were called inalienable.

Using the idea of defining by example natural rights include only these items.

THE RIGHT TO HAVE PROPERTY

This right is inherent to all citizens. This includes those who do not yet own property. It also includes children who have not yet achieved a full citizen status. Just as importantly, the government cannot be allowed to simply dictate the conditions under which property can be taken away without due process of law.

This has an effect on the way we use technology. Your personal information is also your property. Thus, the right to your personal information is yours alone. The government is responsible to protect your electronic information just like your house or your car. When they keep your information on file, the government seems to believe this right does not apply to them.

THE RIGHT TO BELIEVE WHAT YOU WANT AND EXPRESS YOUR BELIEFS

Some early European immigrants consisted of people looking to get away from the Old World. They thought that distance would let them worship God in the way they wanted. By having an ocean between the Old World and themselves, they hoped that this was not something that government would take away. For later immigrants religious beliefs and economic needs became mixed as the reasons they wanted a new life. That is why some of the colonies were based on specific religious groups. Catholics went to Maryland, Quakers immigrated to Pennsylvania. Each religious group seemed to have a preferred location to keep the nonbelievers away. By 1791 this had changed. Separate religious beliefs between colonies had become a mix of beliefs within a colony. In some ways the range of beliefs forced the Constitution to be a compromise. As a result, the original Constitution ended up as a compromise that there would be no state sponsored religion. That way, everyone was free to practice according to their own religious beliefs.

This compromise was later clarified by the Supreme Court in several cases. The first cases reinforced that separation. Later cases limited support for one set of religious beliefs over another. Now it appears that some Supreme Court cases limit free speech under the cover of separating church and state.

The ability to express your beliefs has long been considered one of the strengths of this country. Unfortunately, limiting freedom of religion is not the only type of speech that is now limited.

Examples of other types of limits on expression are almost always offensive to a large segment of the population. I personally find hate speech abominable. In some places hate speech is illegal. Others claim the political speech must be curtailed in the interests of fairness, because money is flooding out small voices in our communications media. It's interesting that it doesn't flood out their voices however. Still others claim that the tea party must be stopped and even used the IRS to try to cut off their views.

Make no mistake, freedom of expression is always under attack when others get to judge what is correct for us to hear. What they are really saying is that they should be able to judge what others can say.

Just as in 1791, there is a real need today to be more explicit in having the law support freedom of expression. This is especially true, since both medicine and technology are changing. Today we can actually take a pill that will make us more charitable. Tomorrow, it is even more likely that we can control what people think. That would be beyond any wild nightmares of the founding fathers.

THE RIGHT TO ASSOCIATE WITH OTHERS IN THE WAY THAT YOU CHOOSE

The right to associate with whom you choose is tightly linked with the right to express your beliefs. You can clearly see the right of association in those situations where the right is being denied. Courts have ruled that the right to congregate is not without controls. Needing to have a permit to march is one example. But when you constrain where and how people may associate, the risk is high that the controls will abuse the rights.

That is part of the reason why this is considered a natural right. The other part is that you must be able to freely join together in groups. If you do not naturally have freedom of association, then all governments including the US government have no foundation in anything other than force. Some people claim that all governments are by nature coercive. However, so long as there is also the natural right of freedom of action, then freedom of association must also be a natural right.

RIGHT OF FREEDOM OF ACTION

How can you be free if you cannot exercise your will in the decisions and actions of your life? That is why Freedom of Action is a natural right. One of the primary purposes of government is to use law to balance between our rights. No freedom can exist that is completely unconstrained for one individual at the expense of another's freedom. That is why that a significant portion of the law is to limit freedom of actions which abridge the rights of others. It is also why a large portion of the law is to insure the freedom of action of individuals.

It is not usually considered this way but "freedom of action" is at the heart of one of the most intense public debates of our time. Unfortunately I cannot conceive another way of expressing this next natural right than what it is, The Right to Life.

THE RIGHT TO LIFE

The term "Right to Life" immediately causes arguments. It is now a slogan in the abortion debate. "Pro-choice" and "Pro-Life" are now rallying cries. These slogans have reached the point of stopping people from reasoning together, or even reaching a rational reasonable conclusion. For that reason, I can only ask that you read the following in its denotative sense, that is the ways the words are defined not the feelings they give us.

I use the term "right to life" in one sense only. People have a right to continue to live just because of their existence. I do not use it to express a position within a highly emotional debate.

I am attempting to stay out of that debate, except for what the debate fails to recognize. One of the beneficial purposes of good government is to insure that when rights conflict, there is a reasonable balance in the law protecting both rights to the degree possible.

We would do better if we had that great debate based on the idea of the law being a balancer of rights. It is actually in that balancing of rights that we should be addressing that debate.

For the moment, let's just agree that the purpose of this book is not about abortion. There are enough new ways of looking at things in this book to cause liberals and conservatives to stop reading.

It is an important topic, just not in the context of defining rights. Its importance would be better served if it was debated in the context of balancing rights, rather than yelling slogans.

Hopefully you will continue reading long enough to read about the last of the natural rights, The Right to Privacy.

THE RIGHT OF PRIVACY

This was the only one of the natural rights which was just in the original bill of rights. Amendment 4 about search and seizure comes close, but it does not really describe a right of privacy.

For more than 150 years after the country was founded, the right of privacy did not exist as an expressed right. But, if you think about it, either there is no right to privacy, or it is a natural right.

What do these five natural rights have in common? These natural rights are not dependent on the law for their existence, but are a natural condition of man. If anything, government and the law are created to insure that individuals keep these rights, and to balance these rights between individuals when conflicts occur.

This leads to what some people consider to be the last of the natural rights. Others consider it the first of the constitutional rights. I've kept it under natural rights since all constitutional rights can only be fairly balanced if this right is assumed to exist.

THE RIGHT TO EQUAL TREATMENT UNDER THE LAW

The US was founded on the principal that all men are created equal. We should realize that a well-formed government requires that all men have the right to equal treatment within the law. This is especially true of a government which is in theory, for the people.

CONSTITUTIONAL RIGHTS

Most of the Constitution described rights in terms of the states and the federal government. Individual rights were only stated in the bill of rights. Later amendments clarified some of these rights or corrected and extended those rights. These included:

218

FREEDOM TO PETITION THE GOVERNMENT (FROM AMENDMENT 1)

The First Amendment was mostly about our natural rights. But it also had one constitutional right, the right to petition the government.

RIGHT TO KEEP AND BEAR ARMS (AMENDMENT 2)

Some people say this amendment only applies to the people in terms of a militia. The reality is this was a right guaranteed to each person as a person. If the government had the right to approve or disapprove a militia, it also had the right to disband it. If that were true, how could a single person still keep and bear arms.

FREEDOM FROM FORCED BILLETING (AMENDMENT 3)

Perhaps this was in the constitution because of an abuse of power by the English government. Perhaps it was simply a knee jerk reaction to that abuse. Whatever the initial reason this is a constitutional right. It is consistent with the concept that a person who owns property should control the use of the property.

FREEDOM FROM SEARCH AND SEIZURE AND FREEDOM FROM WARRANTLESS SEARCHES (AMENDMENT 4)

Only the warrant can force a process to protect a person from the government. It is the process which essentially forces the government to be limited by the process. It is the warrant which protects power from being unleashed without redress.

RIGHTS COMBINED INTO AMENDMENT 5

Amendment 5 includes several different rights. That includes the rights to a Grand Jury for capital charges. It includes freedom from double jeopardy. It also includes freedoms from self -incrimination, and provides a right to Due Process. It protects people through the Rights to Just compensation for property and services take by the government.

This group of rights was a result of several things. In some states, processes of law were being ignored. In other states the process varied widely between states. It became necessary to spell out the rights to insure that they would not be lost. This amendment and the ones which follow read more like requirements documents than the first several amendments.

AMENDMENT 6 RIGHTS

In all criminal prosecution, the accused shall enjoy the right to a speedy and public trial, by an impartial jury of the State and district wherein the crime shall have been committed, which district shall have been previously ascertained by law, and to be informed of the nature and cause of the accusation; to be confronted with the witnesses against him; to have compulsory process for obtaining witnesses in his favor, and to have the Assistance of Counsel for his defense.

AMENDMENT 7

In Suits at common law, where the value in controversy shall exceed twenty dollars, the right of trial by jury shall be preserved, and no fact tried by a jury, shall be otherwise re-examined in any Court of the United States, than according to the rules of the common law. (Amendment 7)

AMENDMENT 8

Excessive bail shall not be required, nor excessive fines imposed, nor cruel and unusual punishments inflicted.

AMENDMENT 9

The enumeration in the Constitution, of certain rights, shall not be construed to deny or disparage others retained by the people. (Amendment 9)

AMENDMENT 10

The powers not delegated to the United States by the Constitution, nor prohibited by it to the states, are reserved to the states respectively, or to the people.

While both of the last two amendments to the bill of rights are directed to the people, they really deal not as much with defining the rights of the individual as they originally addressed limiting the rights of the federal government. It is this lack of specificity, that has colored much of US jurisprudence and legislation since the constitution was originally approved.

Sprinkled throughout the remainder of the amendments to the constitution were those amendments which round out the natural and constitutional right of the individual.

These include several amendments to provide for the abolition of slavery, amendments intended to insure the right to vote for all people (including women, and freed slaves, and those 18 years and older).

Also within the constitutional rights is the very clear example of how constitutional rights can be removed. This was the ill-advised amendments where prohibition was first passed, and then was repealed.

Despite the fact that the constitution has less than 30 amendments, there are yet two additional categories of "rights" in the most general sense. These included Entitlements and Adjudicated Rights.

ENTITLEMENTS

Entitlements are rights which exist only because they were enacted by government. An entitlement can also be repealed by government. That's why caution is needed when entitlements are treated as permanent things. Great care is needed when creating a new entitlement.

Sometimes people consider entitlements to be sacred. Fact is, they are not. Entitlements can be repealed through legislation. Natural rights exist whether there is a government or not.

Do not conclude that I'm speaking only about some kinds of entitlements. I'm actually talking about all kinds of entitlements.

There should always be concerns about adding, changing, or terminating entitlements. While it may be a necessary and even beneficial action, it nevertheless generally infringes on someone rights. That's true even if it's only to pay for the entitlement, since some people pay for things that they do not receive in equal measure.

This then leads to the last rightful source of the "rights" of people, called adjudicated or case law.

ADJUDICATED RIGHTS (OR CASE LAW)

Every right which was first defined as being an individual right through court rulings and decisions is by definition an adjudicated right. The right to privacy and a woman's right to choose were by the nature of the way they were described initially obvious examples of adjudicated rights. There are more, but the point is that these adjudicated rights are just as real as natural and constitutional types of rights.

CONCLUSION

All of the above can easily lead to the question, is whether all rights has equal importance? While it may be possible to rank them, it's likely that this ranking will be more a reflection on the person doing the ranking that any inherent hierarchy of rights and freedoms.

Within those four basic categories, government functions tend to protect the Natural and Constitutional rights with greater vigor and as we progress through the legislated to case law rights, the enforcement appears to decline.

As mentioned previously, one of the most significant roles of government is to be both the protector of these rights and at least in theory the arbiter when rights are in conflict.

It is paramount that no matter what other changes are introduced in Government 2.0 that those rights be protected so that the people in need of those rights are protected as well.

With those principles in mind the next chapter describes a few of the likely changes recommended to better protect these rights.

CHAPTER 17. OTHER IMPORTANT REQUIREMENTS

If you treat individual rights as requirements, there are some questions that just jump out demanding an answer. Why do we treat things differently when some people are denied their rights? Sometimes it seems to be different based on whose rights were denied. Sometimes it seems to be different depending on who is denying the rights. Sometimes it seems to be different depending on which right is violated.

The last 250 years has been a history of redefining civil rights. Each time we redefine those rights, we must change the process to defend those rights. Each time we change the process we must make changes to support that process. This is a classic case of a system made weaker over time by not having changes be well designed.

The federal government has always taken actions to arbitrate, mitigate, subvert or enable the wider distribution of the individual rights. Sometimes these changes occurred *without* legislative, state, or judicial authorization but always with executive branch support.

Each change to the definition occurred either within the framework of the system or more often outside the normal framework. The history of civil rights is strewn with executive orders which either extended, or denied civil rights. Each of those orders contributed to the chaos within the system today.

When a president acts without pre-approval from the Congress to expand, or limit or change the protections of these rights, the president was at least wrong on process. Sometimes a president was wrong on principal as well. Roosevelt's orders regarding US born Japanese is one example of that.

But civil rights generally was expanded through executive order much more commonly than through legislation. Here are just three examples. Kennedy ordered federal law enforcement to implement school desegregation. Lincoln suspended the writ of habeas corpus. Obama issued the Dream Act Executive Order. Each of these did not wait for congressional approval.

One requirement for Gov 2.0 should include a way to quickly bring and resolve cases involving people's rights. The legal system has long had civil rights law. But when you look closer, the law has been a series of amendments and patches to other laws. There has never been a clear description of how loss of rights should be judged and what appropriate penalties are. This is a result of how individual rights were slowly understood and added to our legal system.

With Gov 2.0 we can make our system work better to protect individual rights and freedoms. We can make the process more precise by acting against individuals who break the law. We don't need to make every civil rights case a multi-year effort. Each case doesn't need to involve millions of dollars. We can make it more effective, and quicker to reach a fair judgment.

Here are some examples of what can occur because we don't actually look to balance people's actions and their rights. These are examples that the design of Gov 2.0 should fix.

CLEAR CIVIL RIGHTS REQUIREMENTS

HIDING EVIDENCE

There are times when a few bad police officers hide evidence from the defense attorneys intentionally. It seems to me that act is always illegal. Yet, most of the time the penalties against the policeman are civil actions. If it even is publicized you hear about suspensions, or reduced rank, and in really bad cases, being fired. You never hear about actual criminal charges.

IMPROPER PROCEDURE

Harry is arrested for armed robbery and rape. For whatever reason, the police failed to follow procedure and obtain a search warrant when they went through his apartment. Because of that error, Harry is able to get his case thrown out of court. The officers involved in making the mistake usually aren't punished. To be fair, perhaps a few are punished without publicity. Bur the person who was robbed and raped also had their rights denied by Harry. Because of that mistake they get no justice either.

CLASS ACTION VERSUS CRIMINAL ACTION

Remember the story of Jerry Smallwood and a new job in a new town from the Forward? That story ended with

Jerry feeling more comfortable about his new apartment and his new city.

In today's world, in Government 1.5 the swift resolution of his complaint is not going to happen. It's not even theoretically possible. Today because we have no practical way of treating these kinds of issues locally, the problem is either ignored (fanning more discontent) or elevated to a national debate (thus fanning the flames even more).

Today the only option Jerry has is to file suit against the apartment management company. That may end up being financially beneficial in a small number of cases. But is always seems to hurt innocents on the company side (like Sally). And it doesn't actually fix the problem. Because Jerry really can't effectively file suit against Fred who definitely appeared to be abridging his rights, he has no recourse, and frankly makes it likely that these types of actions continue unopposed in far too many instances.

Denying an individual their natural rights is the same type of action. It's the severity of the denial that needs to be judged. There must be a basis to determine whether there is a penalty. And there must be a scale to judge the size of the penalty. And yet, when have you heard of an individual being charged with just discrimination? It's always been treated as a crime of a group, company, government, club, or society.

Intentional denial of rights is ALWAYS a crime by at least one person. It always affects at least one person. Sometimes you have groups of people who act together as a mob or a gang, but you always have at least one person acting against another.

Unintentionally denying rights is not necessarily a crime. Sometimes it's that the person is just incompetent. This is especially true of people who decide whether someone should receive an entitlement.

An individual should have the right to bring charges against an individual for all actions which affect their rights. Judges and magistrates should be the people who decide whether the action was intentional. Courts should decide whether it really was a material infringement of their rights.

Government, at all levels, has the **responsibility** to bring criminal charges against an individual for all actions which intentionally deny someone their rights. Failure to do so is by definition a second crime. Remember abridging the person's right for equal treatment under the law?

Some readers will say you cannot treat the denial of all rights as a criminal not a civil lawsuit. They will claim that there are at least two problems.

The first problem is that nobody sues someone who is broke. A civil suit allows for a settlement at times worth millions of dollars. This criticism is actually a good reason to treat criticism at the individual level. It seems that direct action against those who deny rights is more effective as a deterrent.

The second problem was that any chance like this would swamp the courts. Here again, this is actually a reason to design changes into the court system. A way to improve the speed of delivery of government's basic services including legal services is another legitimate and appropriate design level goal if Government 2.0 were to ever be designed, developed, and even partially implemented.

LIMITING GOVERNMENT ABUSE REQUIREMNTS

Government is the responsible group to enforce and protect rights. But that responsibility has a very high risk. Government must have the right tools to protect all of our rights. But those same tools opens a way for people in government to abuse their power. Examples are sprinkled throughout our history that show this. In some examples, the failure was to enforce rights. In others it was outright use of power to deny rights. But it was not only the direct rights that were injured. There was also injury to the willingness of people to participate and be the real source of government. I live in a neighborhood where the police are viewed as both friend and the enemy. It is because of the history of that abuse of power, that people do not look to the police as a protector so much as an enforcer.

By designing in limits to power we can reduce the government abuse of those tools. We can limit the way government can turn that protection into a means of coercion.

Perhaps a more general directed requirements concerning abuse, is that Gov 2.0 must design the protection of all people's rights more effectively than the government which we have today.

INDIVIDUAL PRIVACY REQUIREMENTS

In order to protect the rights of the individual, the US government is presented with a problem, that is, the right to privacy itself.

Privacy by its nature in today's society includes the electronic identify that we all have. We have our personal information on our home systems. We have copies or shadows of it in many public and government systems. We've now gotten to where the government uses acronyms like PII and FTI. [18] These buzzwords have become short hand for the data the government has about people. These terms set the ways that the government expects the data to be handled. These ways supposedly are to protect people's rights from access by those OUTSIDE the government.

Unfortunately, the government has not done much to protect the information from people INSIDE the government. We've fallen into the ownership trap. The ownership trap is the belief that a person's electronic information belongs to the government. It's easy to see why this happened. Government not only received it, they needed to assemble it. They also had to store it. The real information age was only in its infancy. PII data is actually at a minimum part of your electronic identity. That is, it really is your information not the governments. The methods and ways that they access your data should remain under your control. Today it most certainly is not. Today it most certainly can be.

---

18 PII stands for Personal Identifying Data and FTI stands for Federal Tax Information.

From a broad design view, the right of the individual to privacy requires major changes from both the individual and the government. We need to make sure that the government only uses our information appropriately. Government needs to change the design of its systems to be sure the person's electronic information is not misused.

Since most of us have been raised in the information age, most people have at least a minor concern that the government may be accessing your information without your knowledge. For most people there is at least an acceptance that people in government can access your information without your explicit permission. Given today's technology, given what has been described in this book, it's obvious that it doesn't have to stay that way.

Gov 2.0 must insure that a person's individual data remains under the person's control. This is the basic privacy requirement.

INDIVIDUAL RIGHTS AT THE COMMUNITY LEVEL

As a society we've used many different ways to try to protect people's rights. In some instances[19] we make the infraction dependent on the specific condition under which the action occurs. We can point to examples for civil rights. We can see different rules for government contractors and government employees.

---

19 Example USC 18 242-248

Different rules exist for how you can earn or lose voting rights. Some employment rights vary by state. The list of such variations is very long.

You may remember the simple view expressed earlier in this chapter that:

Government at all levels must insure protection of the rights of all individuals without regards to who they are, who they know, how they look, what they think, and what they say, or how much money and power they have. This was coupled with the following:

A person being actively denied their rights is a crime by a person or persons against other person or persons. In every single case, it is a crime against people by people.

This is obviously not the situation today.

Some instances of individual rights being denied are severe, some are just painful, and some are completely disregarded.

Generally the concept of a constitutional amendment becomes attractive for these far-reaching kinds of changes, but in reality a relatively simple piece of legislation could address these requirements. The Federal Individual Rights Enforcement Act in Volume II describes what such a bill could look like, based on the framework of what this chapter contains.

RIGHTS AS REQUIREMENTS SUMMARY

At the time of the initial publication of the Constitution, only some rights were protected by the constitution.

This resulted in the first 9 amendments. These amendments were to insure the protection of these natural rights and constitutional rights. And then there were those created later from case law. Right such as the right to privacy "created from penumbras and emanations" which may be said for both the description of the right, and the mind of the justice who penned the phrase. Most of these rights are still not treated like "natural" rights.

There is another large change to our ideas of individual rights. We have also changed who was "eligible" to even have natural rights.

Some people will ask if our natural rights have changed over the last 225 years. Others will say we recognized a natural right that already existed. Frankly, it does not make a difference. What's important is that it is agreed upon that these are not even presumed rights, they are indelibly guaranteed rights. Without that level of guarantee, the authority of the government to ignore, abridge or downgrade these rights will always be an even greater opportunity for loss of those freedoms than any action by individuals could possibly be.

CHAPTER 18. FINAL THOUGHTS AND COMING ATTRACTIONS

If you are reading this I very much admire your perseverance. That is especially true if you aren't a friend or a member of my family.

Of course it is possible that you being paid to do this as part of opposition research. In fact, I hope you are being paid to read this. It means I'm having at least a little impact. This is partially why I started running for office. If you are, I can only hope I've managed to make you think about switching sides.

Just because you've read the book doesn't make it a success even though you made it this far. But if what I've written makes you begin to think about how we can make government work better (not work for me, nor work against you or me), then the book is a success.

If you disagree with what I've written, please let me know why.[20] I don't take offense at criticisms. At least I don't object to critiques based on fact. I even enjoy hearing opinions that are opposed to mine so long as you respect my right to an opinion as well as yours. Please submit them to Steve@SteveImholt.com

Who knows, perhaps you can change my mind.

---

20 Comments regarding my ancestry, my parentage, or especially my progeny do little to engage in meaningful discussion, so I would ask that you please refrain from it. I don't treat any of those kinds of characterizations of my work as actual critiques but rather as attempts to avoid thinking about what I've written. And yes, I'm afraid I too am stereotyping, but most likely those types of attacking comments are because I didn't adhere to your notions of what we should be doing about our future.

I've been asked why I didn't spend as much time on how we can improve on our government delivery systems for states, and non-government organizations. Fact is though, I believe changes at those levels will only be permanent if we first make the federal government work better for people.

If you have observations or suggestions on improving the ideas in this book please send them to input@SteveImholt.com.

WHY DID I WRITE GOVERNMENT 2.0

Anyone who has worked with me professionally, knows that I've said solutions are what IT is. I've said something like the following too many times to count.

"Raising a problem or issue, or concern, is a good first step. It's even better to raise the problem and recommend a solution."

After the last decades spent building systems and working with people in and out of government, I've concluded that there are deep problems in our government systems. These problems are a result of complex critical issues. I am concerned that if we do not address these problems it will likely cost us our freedoms. This may not happen completely within my lifetime, but it certainly will within my children's.

I've grown tired of political campaigns with no meaning. I no longer believe promises that are impossible to keep. I hate tactics that should make any candidate be ashamed of what has occurred in politics.

So rather than simply gripe with no suggestions or quietly watch the world go to hell in a hand basket or go out and scream at rallies, I thought I'd try something very different. I'd try to take my own advice, and offer some suggestions.

Those suggestions quickly grew into a set of related concepts. These concepts forced me to start looking at the problems the same way I look at business systems. As I wrote and expanded on that, I began to see a way for information technology to help solve the problems that its existence has helped create. Information Technology can be a way to move past the gritted teeth campaigning, polling and instant analysis to something that I would actually like to hear more about.

As I've neared completion of this book, I kept seeing news briefs, articles, and commentary that would be affected by the ideas in this book. Some of the changes would be minor, but others like the commentary on racism would be a in a completely different tone. Racism is a local problem. It has to be solved at the local level. The concept of applying justice at the local level perhaps will make real equality possible.

Here is an example of what I mean about separating roles in the executive branch. I read just yesterday, that there is an effort initiated by some of the Federal Election Commission members. They want to censor electronic media before an election. That effort (even if nothing comes of it), is just the latest example of why you cannot give the same group of people the power to set regulations, and to determine whether those regulations are fair and just.

So in brief, the reasons that I wrote this book are in decreasing order of priority.

First, I think my children and grandchildren deserve better than the mess their parents have created in the forms of government, and the forms of political discourse.

Second, I do think this country is able to both change, and improve for everyone's benefits if someone were to actually make intelligent suggestions.

Third, I think buried within these scribbling are just a couple of those suggestions.

Fourth, my family got tired of listening to me talk about these things one at a time.

COMING ATTRACTIONS

VOLUME 2 – DESIGN AND IMPLEMENTATION PLANNING

The second volume in the series[21] describes a way to beyond the architecture and design in this book. It shows one way to develop detail designs. It shows a way to use those designs and begin to produce a set of implementation plans.

---

21 By the time this book is published, it has become very apparent that more than one additional book is required. So some of the items described here may in fact be carried in those subsequent volumes.

It has chapters that describe:

- Possible legislative and congressional changes including potential Constitutional Amendments

- Descriptions of the programs, projects and rollout plan vision for Government 2.0

- State and Local Government Impacts and Options .If these first two volumes provide any tangible benefits to the body politic, the State and Local Government impacts could be expanded to its own set of volumes

- Approaches to Costing have some suggestions on how to cost the overall program. By no means should anyone think that this is a final cost estimate at this stage of the architecture.

- Going from theory to reality has some thoughts on how to actually begin and move forward with the re-architecture of Government 2.0

This second volume will lag behind the first volume in being published because the second volume really does demand effort by a larger number of people. Otherwise, the domain can shift while you still are in detail design.

If you think the ideas here are worth discussing more especially if you consider yourself technically oriented, please contact me at steve@steveimholt.com

MAKING A VISION REALITY

I think most people are like my family. They are tired of politicians, wonks, writers and professional gripers. They are tired of pundits and candidates yelling about how the other group is wrong. Most of all they are tired of no one ever really telling you what they can do to address the issues of the day.

I am still idealistic enough to believe that change is possible. I am also realistic. I know that without substantial participation from many people, no change will occur.

The two books, Vision and Volume 2 – Design and Implementation Planning, both contain one huge assumption. They assume that the vision has been sold. That is obviously not the case. The Sale of the vision must precede the implementation.

Some simple lessons I've learned in software development the hard way. Here are a few.

In order for the system to be implemented, it must first be designed.

In order for it to be designed, the users must both understand the new system and accept the changes that a new system brings.

In order for a new system to be understood and accepted, sometimes, you must first be sold on the need and merits of the system.

For the new system to be successful the sale of the vision must precede the implementation.

These books can help with that understanding both of the need, and the merits. I believe these books can begin a conversation that inevitably ends in a force to drive towards implementation and acceptance.

Fortunately, the effort to go from vision to sale only (tongue in cheek) requires only five things.

- o People who believe that these changes are not only needed but are possible
- o A way for people to join together on educating, advocating, and organizing the effort to make the changes such a system requires.
- o Individuals who are willing to step up and say "Now is the time" through their voices to their friends and their family even at the risk of sounding bombastic.
- o Monetary support for those people of both parties who advocate these kinds of change.
- o Perseverance.

Over the next few months as I continue to look for paying work, I'll be trying to spread the word about Gov 2.0. I'll be doing that mostly by both personal and electronic jawboning.

Right now for example, I'm circulating petitions to have my name placed on the ballot for the Virginia House of Delegates. I'm particularly happy about that, because among the people who have represented this are in the House of Delegates over the last couple hundred years was Patrick Henry.

www.ffeg.org will be another way. It will stand for the Foundation For Effective Government. Why yet another think tank group? I've found that there is simply no group in the Washington maelstrom that actually is trying to make government effective. Seems that agendas push the ideology as the solution, rather than simply a starting point.

www.ffeg.org if the site is established.

Through the second book Government 2.0 Design and Implementation Planning once it is published.

www.SteveImholt.com once that site is open for business.

I want to thank everyone for taking the time to read and evaluate the contents and approaches recommended through these books.

APPENDICES

APPENDIX A-- ADDITIONAL STORIES

These stories may help to give a better understanding of how Gov 2.0 could work.

THE INDIVIDUAL AND MOVING INTO A NEW FNO

THE STORY – SALLY MOVING OUT AND INTO HER FIRST APARTMENT

Sally has finally moved out of her parent's house! She just signed a lease on a new apartment across town. So Sally goes down to her new FNO and initiates the change of address process. Sally finds operations are very different in her new Center called the Alfred E Newman Center. Her new FNO serves a community which is mostly has college students. Looking at the one page history of the new FNO she sees where the students had overwhelmingly voted for the name when the center was founded, as homage to MAD magazine. It also explains why the hours of operation are from noon to 10PM. The FNO near her parents' house was open 8-6 each day. When Sally registers at her new FNO the FNO customer service initiates a couple of standard processes. These are to help Sally get her electronic PDS and Federal ID to be relocated as well.

DESCRIPTION OF THE ADDRESS CHANGE PROCESS THROUGH THE FNO

One pain in the neck piece of every move is telling all the different groups and companies that you have moved. One of the standard processes that each FNO Center has is a relocation confirm service. The relocation confirm service starts with a Customer Service representative reviewing your change of address. They then confirm you are who you say you are. They then allow the change in address to the government linkages to your PDS based on address. The FNO software will automatically notify the prior location FNO of your move. The old FNO then takes actions to "close up" your relationship with the old FNO. For example, if you had already recorded votes on issues that haven't yet finished voting, those as yet uncounted FNO votes will be purged in the old FNOs voting support system.

When a person moves into a states which uses the new Federal Electronic Voting Service (FEVS) several more things happen. The States Board of Elections is notified of the new location for them. If that person is a registered voter in the same state, the Voter Registration Process will notify the voter of their new district, precinct, or legislative area. If they are not, an email will be sent inviting them to become a registered voter in the new state. If the person was from out of state his original State would be notified that he had moved out of state. That way the old state can be notified to remove the person from the voting roles.

Utilities and State Agencies can also be notified of the individual's departure and/or arrival at the new address.

THE AMISH AND THE PERSONAL DATA STORE EMAIL SYSTEM

THE STORY - INGRID HERGVOLD AND HER NEED FOR FNO SUPPORT

Ingrid is Amish and she doesn't want to use the new technologies. She and her family have all asked the FNO to print their mail. That way it can be physically delivered or they will come to pick it up. So, the FNO prints all her emails and includes it with the physical mail. It is then delivered by the local GAA delivery vendor. Ingrid is charged a monthly fee for the service unless she can show that her income level causes her fee to be waived. The same waiver of the fee would be available if Ingrid is disabled and unable to use the email service.

DESCRIPTION OF THE VARIABILITY OF SERVICES FOR THE FNO

Most areas will have a need for some email to be printed. That way the service can work for those who cannot actually receive their own email. FNO operations GAAs would normally expect to budget in some hours for supporting that function. But in some areas, such as rural Pennsylvania, and Ohio, where there are many Amish, there would be a need to budget more hours (and even more people) to support a specific community need.

THE INDIVIDUAL - FEDERAL AND STATE VOTING

THE STORY WILLIAM AND WILLA VOGT (FROM THE FORWARD)

Both Willa and Will are retired, and tend to lose track of the days.

When Will checks his email he gets a reminder that today is Election Day in their state, California. Because California uses the Federal Electronic Voting System (FEVS), they can vote directly from home. Using the FEVS system, they are directed to the California ballot for their location. There they can vote on elections for office holders. In their case that would include the local public Waste Management Board and the local FNO Board election)

When they complete their voting, FEVS updates their voting record and their PDS. That way the system has a record that they had now voted.

DESCRIPTION OF THE FEDERAL ELECTRONIC VOTING SYSTEM

The Federal Electronic Voting System is a new feature for elections at both the state and federal levels. It really is just an extension of the same system used for FNO voting. It makes it easy for people to both securely vote. It also makes it easy to be sure that people only vote once in the areas where they are authorized to vote.

THE CONVICT, HIS HISTORY AND THE FNO FEDERAL ADVOCATE

As the individual's info is centralized state arrest and conviction history could easily be combined. They would each become another set of folders within the government wing. This has several obvious benefits. First, each state could access the individual's arrest history from within their state or other states. This is been designed to actually record as part of legitimate law enforcement activity. Secondly, the individual can more easily initiate and manage the effort to get his history expunged. Third, in those cases where identity theft had been involved, unknowing victims can become aware of where and when it occurred.

THE STORY - JAMES AND HIS DRUNK AND DISORDERLY COLLEGE DAYS

James in his younger days was arrested for drunk and disorderly along with resisting arrest while attending Indiana University 15 years before. The State of Indiana has just agreed to copy their conviction records to the people who have a PDS as part of the Federal Conviction History Project. When James gets a notice that the State of Indiana has accessed his government conviction history, and subsequently posted it to his legal records in his Government Wing, James immediately logs in to see what is being recorded.

Along with that notice he received from the logging function, is some cryptic legal jabber that says something about conditions to be met before his record can be expunged.

James goes into his local FNO and asks for some help with understanding the government notice. At the FNO, the Federal Advocate first calms James down, then tells him that since Indiana is participating in the national conviction history program, they also have agreed to allow electronic requests for reviews and potential expunging of records if Indiana's specific criteria have been met. Looking over the Indiana State criteria, the Federal Advocate verifies that it appears all the specific criteria have been met which means that not only James can electronically petition to have his record cleared, but also that it's likely to be approved. The advocate assists James in filing the request, and includes his recommendation that the request be granted.

Four weeks later James receives another email where he finds that the State of Indiana has granted his petition, his records have been accessed and his Indiana legal history has now been expunged since all criteria have been met.

He also receives another email from his Federal Advocate congratulating him on the record being expunged, and reminding him that he is now eligible to vote should he decide to register.[22]

DESCRIPTION OF THE INDIVIDUAL
CONVICTION HISTORY

---

22 The only reason the Federal Advocate had been notified about the change was that the advocate had recommended that the record be expunged.

The Federal Arrest Conviction Project is an optional state program that allows States to join the Federal Conviction Registry, as well as sets the minimum conditions through which the records may be expunged. In turn the Federal Conviction Registry has the responsibility to update the Individuals Conviction History[23] within the Government Wing of the individuals PDS.

Refer to Section 1.7.10 for more information regarding the Individual Conviction History.

DESCRIPTION OF THE FNO FEDERAL ADVOCATE

In setting up the FNO Center legislation, one of the FNO personnel to be included within the standard facility staffing plan is a Federal Advocate who has been specifically trained to assist in a number of different areas, including helping to understand and deal with the variety of notifications that individuals in the community receive about their governments actions that affect them. The Federal Advocate is specifically trained to be able to offer information about these areas, and to support the individual in the steps they need to take to receive a specific service, or specific

---

23 The Federal Individual Conviction History within the individuals PDS is one of the few items where there is an intentional duplication of federal records. It is not intended that this replace those records retained by the Federal Courts, or the FBI, or any other criminal recording. What it is intended to do, is to allow the history of the individual to be available quickly when there is a legitimate reason for accessing it. As with all other accesses, a logging in the individuals PDS would occur automatically except in the case of a court order.

action from a wide variety of executive branch agencies, GAAs and even states who elect to use the FNOs for supporting some of their services.

THE INDIVIDUAL AND THE US POSTAL SERVICE

One of the few functions directly described within the Constitution was the idea of a Postal Service. For the last two hundred years, that function has been performed by the US Postal Service. With the advent of email the basic nature of the US Postal service should have begun an evolution into the email age. Given the decreasing volume of traditional mail, the political hazards of closing post offices, and the overarching belief that the USPS should only provide a limited number of services, there is ample reason to support an actual significant redesign of the US Postal Service. Here is one example of how a re-engineered USPS could work.

THE STORY OF JOHNNY, HIS MOM AND THE MAIL

When Johnny got home from school this afternoon, he notices a package on the side of the front steps which was dropped off earlier in the day by FedEx. Since FedEx now delivers mail for his FNO, he knows any physical mail they might have is also there, so he checks the mailbox, and as expected, found nothing. Most mail now comes via email, so even the 3 day a week delivery schedule often doesn't seem necessary.

Putting it on the kitchen table, he uses his cell phone to open his PDS to review any emails he had received including any US Postal Service electronic mail. Most of what he gets this way, is pretty much the same content he used to get in the mailbox, flyers for 10% off everything in the store, life insurance policies (even though he was only 15)[24] . He then sees the letter sitting on the kitchen table. Now he remembers his mom telling him to put the letter in the mailbox as he left this morning. "Uh Oh" he says now trying to figure out how to cover his mistake.

While he could have put the letter in the mailbox to be picked up by the letter carrier two days from now, he decides to take the letter down to the FNO and get it on its way, so he doesn't run the risk of having his mom notice he hadn't gotten the letter into the mail.

When he gets to the FNO, he sees that the barcode printer is open, so he uses the keypad to address it to his brother who now lives out of town. He puts the sticker on the letter and since he knows it will go out that night it'll keep him out of trouble.

DESCRIPTION OF US POSTAL SERVICE CHANGES

This story is an example of several of the changes for the US postal service. First, by establishing a PDS for each individual, and having an email set up for each individual (either by the individual or by the FNO on behalf of the individual), significant portions of the

---

24 It is not reasonable to expect that a new delivery mechanism will correct all mail issues, especially content.

remaining snail mail distributed by the US Postal Service can be redirected to the email counterpart to the physical mailbox.

The US Postal Service changes would also include the transference of all normal post office substation and station functions to the Federal Neighborhood Office with the exception of home delivery which would be offered by subcontracts to delivery GAAs.

Delivery of physical mail would be reduced to 3 times weekly, and all local post offices would be closed.

Further details can be found in Section 1.7.11.

A CITIZEN AND HIS MEDICAL RECORD

In addition to the obvious benefit to the VA of having a medical record system that works, the benefit to the general population as a whole can be almost as beneficial.

The Story - Chuck and his Electronic Medical RECORD

Chuck gets an email on his cell phone from his physician about needing his annual checkup. The note includes a request to allow the physician to access to his electronic medical record from his Personal Data Store (PDS), along with a link to his physician's office schedule.

Going to his Amazon Personal Data Store (PDS), Chuck accesses the Healthcare wing of his PDS, selects his Electronic Medical Record, and then flags it with a temporary sharable pass code which he can send back to the physician. When finished he uses the link to go to the physician office schedule to select an appointment which he selects and provides the sharable pass code.

DESCRIPTION OF THE INDIVIDUAL'S MEDICAL RECORD

Part of the individuals Personal Data Store (PDS) is an area for medical records. The Medical Record wing will be able to be accessed only when the owner of the PDS authorizes a health care provider, and then only for the period of time that the PDS owner specifies. Refer to Section 2.02 for more information regarding the PDS.

PUBLIC FUNDING OF PDS AND THE FEDERAL ID CARD AS A DEBIT CARD

For decades, the Federal and State governments along with people across the country have engaged in debates about whether people should have ID cards for accessing of certain government functions usually the right to vote. Given the nature of the changes in the government that come with Government 2.0, there is a need for ALL people to have government issued ID cards at the federal level to provide (and control) access to government services AND to provide a consistent access to individuals Personal Data Stores.

THE STORY - JOHAN SCHMIDT AND HIS FEDERAL IDENTIFICATION CARD

Johan makes heavy use of his Personal Data Store (PDS) operated by HP.

Since Johan lost his job a couple of months back, he hasn't been able to pay for his full Personal Data Store. Nevertheless, because the government now provides a minimal PDS for those who can't pay or who do not wish to open a complete PDS, the government wing in his electronic house is still accessible. Johan has been making heavy use of his PDS in recording in his UTDWS information in his PDS and reporting to the State of Utah Department of Workforce Services (UTDWS)[25] his efforts to find work. Since Utah is one of the states that utilizes the Government PDS for individual storage, his UTDWS would be stored within the government wing as do the IRS, SSA, and VA information from the federal level.

Since Johan no longer had a bank account, his Personal Identification Card has been set to allow its use as a debit card. This in turn had allowed the UTDWS to directly deposit to his FIC debit account, the weekly or monthly unemployment compensation payments.

DESCRIPTION OF PUBLIC FUNDING FOR A REDUCED PDS

While the extensions of the Personal Data Store are based on what different vendors decide to package on the Individual Side of the PDS, the government, Medicare, and email wings benefits the population as a whole. While the benefits to the public are in improved security and improved services, for the government, the

---

25 See Chapter 4 State and Local Government Benefits and Impacts

primary benefit is in the resulting ability to have GAAs be contracted to perform some government functions along with marginally reduced costs of storage. As a result, all individuals in the US who cannot or will not pay for a complete PDS will be provided a minimal function PDS with only the capabilities necessary to support effective and efficient government operations while still protecting individuals privacy rights.

The public funding of these reduced data stores will be a single rate per individual levied to the federal government from each GAA PDS vendor, for all individual PDS which have not paid for the service. For each FNO which has individuals who have not paid for the PDS, the individual will be notified by the FNO that they are in a suspended status on their PDS, and the FNO will authorize the payment to the GAA PDS vendor for the total fees unpaid for the government portion of their individuals PDS. The FNO will also notify the individual that they must provide to the FNO that their income level is such that they are unable to pay for the service or they will be fined for failure to pay for the PDS. Once a year in December, the accounts which are still suspended and are able to pay for the service will have the amount past due included as a fee to be reported on the annual income taxes and added to the net taxes due.

The obvious question then is how much of the individuals PDS is actually what used to be called government Personal Data. The following are part of this concept

- All federal agencies storage of individual records within the PDS.

- All U.S. mail email services will continue to function.
- All individual Medical Records will continue to be stored and accessible by health care professionals, and the individual.
- All State agencies information sets which have agreed to store their information within the individuals PDS.
- All individuals access to the tracking logs of the PDS.

For further information refer to 2.02.

APPENDIX B - GLOSSARY

Because of the wide variety of federal and state agencies described within this book, only those terms which are not within the federal lexicon will be described here. For further information for agencies, it is suggested that the reader simple do a public search.

Business Entity - An organization or company who can interact with the US government

EMR – An electronic Medical record for an individual usually housed within the PDS.

Federal Electronic Voting System – An automated service developed and provided by the federal government to insure the accurate, rapid, accumulation and reporting of election results to those state which participate in the FEVS System

FEVS – See Federal Electronic Voting System.

Federal Local Magistrate Court – See Chapter 8.

Federal Neighborhood Office – See Chapter 6.

FIS – Federal Information Office – See Chapter 4.

FLMC – Federal Local Magistrate Court - See Chapter 8.

FNO – Abbreviation for Federal Neighborhood Office. See Chapter 6.

FFNOI – Funding Federal Neighborhood Office Initiatives – possible legislation passed in 2018 which provides a fund to each FNO to be used in the awarding of grants and loans to schools, local government, and civic organization to meet local neighborhood goals and needs.

GAO – Government Accountability Office

Government Accountability Office (GAO) – basically a federal agency which is part of the legislative branch of the government, not the federal branch

Government Authorized Agent (GAA) -- a general term used to describe either an agency or contracted company which has direct access to a specific agency room inside the PDS' of individuals, as well as contracted companies (such as those which provide individual tax completion.

GOV 1.0. This is the name of the first version of the US national government. This version was titled the Confederation of States.

GOV 1.5 This is the name of the second release of the United States National Government. We called this the US Government or the USD Constitution, or just simply the United States of America.

Gov 2.0 This is the name proposed for the efforts to re-engineer, validate, and then implement the architecture described by this book.

Personal Data Store (PDS) – An electronic image of all of a person's government information, usually supplemented by personal information. The PDS resides within the cloud. Further information is available in Chapter 7

Populi – Specific term used for the new branch of the Federal Government described as a possible Article IX of the constitution.

OMB – Office of Management and Budget

Office of Management and Budget – Executive Branch Agency which is responsible for compiling the overall executive budget along with providing recommendations on management practices for other federal agencies

SNAP Program – Supplemental Nutritional Assistance Program

TANSTAAFL – Acronym for **T**here **I**sn't **N**o **S**uch **T**hing **A**s **A** **F**ree **L**unch

APPENDIX C – PERSPECTIVES

Most of the perspectives below are meant to provide clarity to why a particular component is not an attempt to subvert one group over another. Certain perspectives are obviously intended for other purposes, in most cases a humorous purpose.

There is no hidden agenda for this book. If you find you agree with enough of what this book is about to want to know more, or even better participate, please visit the websites listed in Chapter 16 for more information. If you would like to suggest I include your perspective in upcoming books, please email me at Steve@SteveImholt.com.

GOV 2.0 – CONSERVATIVE PERSPECTIVE

The entire book is really about how to merge some of the demands of progressives into a coherent approach. It is not simply to surrender to those demands. The approach itself has an underlying goal of reforming the structure. This will help the American people to regain control of the operations of the government.

In the last century the role of the federal government has grown in ways both intended and unintended. The result is people no longer can have a direct effect on the performance of the government. This book as a whole is the beginning of a road map of how to regain that control. Even better, it does it in a controlled fashion. Through the rejuvenation of neighborhoods, communities can better control their neighborhoods.

They can regain responsibility for the performance of the federal government within those neighborhoods. These results can be profound in all the ways that are most important.

The result of these actions is that local control of how services are delivered will again be possible. This is true even though the programs and procedures are federal in nature. And that local control will cut the higher costs of central administration. This then reduces the power of the bureaucracy to cripple the rights of individuals.

Violating government rules is reduced to the level that is actually appropriate, that is, misdemeanors and fines. It limits rules being used as weapons of the government. So rules are less likely to delay and destroy those who disagree with the government. Rights violations will be much more directly applied. The government then no longer denies both justice and individuals rights.

Some people will attack specific parts of Gov 2.0 as causing bigger government. That isn't true. Returning power to local control is a conservative view. And most components are to support local control. So these new components actually foster more conservative government.

Some conservatives will still claim that Gov 2.0 is anything but an acceptable approach to improve government. They will say that none of it is acceptable to a "real" conservative. For those people, the following sections provide another view of the major components.

THE FEDERAL NEIGHBORHOOD OFFICE IS NOT A PROGRESSIVE PROGRAM

Some of the most important aspects of Gov 2.0 have two counter balanced objectives. For example, the FNO has one objective to more effectively deliver federal services. These services comprise a large piece of the Federal Budget. The FNO moves the delivery of those services to a smaller local level.

As services are moved to the FNOs, duplicate services are eliminated from the old federal system. This reduces the cost of operations.

LETTING ENTREPRENEURSHIP THRIVE

The FNO board is selected by the local community. FNO operations can be mostly done by local businesses selected by the FNO board. This lets the FNO board decide if they want to support small businesses, which is very likely. This then allows those small businesses to compete against larger companies in providing services to the residents. This reduces the influence of big business.

Almost all services provided directly by the FNO are contracted. And there is a potential for wide ranging competition. As a result, unions won't exist at most FNOs. That means that unions will not be able to make local government an extension of the unions.

RESTORING CIVIC PARTICIPATION

The FNO board provides a chance for communities to be involved in government. This helps the local community to take responsibility for the growth and survival of each community across the country. This is in stark contrast to the Federal Executive Branch which tends to ignore local community input.

The FNOs are not an endorsement or critique of any specific service. That is for discussions between conservatives and progressives. But local FNOs are not expected to over reach on government programs as much as happens today.

There will however be one result at the local level that should be welcomed. The impact of progressive self-appointed champions of the people should be reduced.

THE PERSONAL DATA STORE IS NOT A PROGRESSIVE CONCEPT

The reality is that the government has more data about you than it does about most foreign heads of state. Prior to the information age, there really was no alternative. Today however, that does not have to be the case. Instead, your information should be more like an old style bankbook. The old style bankbook let you present it to the authorities, that is the bank. They would then perform their tasks (such as deposits and withdrawals). Now, instead of "presenting" your bankbook, the government will have to request your information from your "banker". In this case the "banker" is your PDS vendor. In turn the PDS vendor has to record the access, the purpose of the access, the agency or GAA who requested the access, and what information they retrieved. In most ways this provides much more control of the individual's information than even the most conservative groups have requested.

The government will keep your data from now on unless something dramatic happens. There appear to be no plans to shut down Social Security. The same is true of Medicare, and the IRS. Each of these programs has your information. And you have no idea who is accessing it. But at least with the PDS approach, you can tell when your information is being accessed, and at least in theory tell what the reason was for the access. This also is a huge improvement on the current environment from just about everyone's point of view, where now you have no idea whether your information is being accessed for good or for ill.

THE FEDERAL ID CARD IS A NECESSARY TOOL NOT A TRACKING DEVICE

Some conservatives believe that some people today take advantage of the system. They believe this happens in a number of ways. One way is through being paid for duplicated services. Another way is when a person defrauds the system using fake or duplicated IDs. They believe it also happens where eligibility is separated from the distribution of funds. The Federal ID Card helps to reduce fraud by making it mandatory to get federal services.

That same thinking applies to a person voting multiple times in a single election. The use of a Federal ID card would clearly eliminate that problem.

It really is the same idea as the original Social Security card. Everyone received a card with a unique Social Security Number. This is taking that idea and extending it to the 21st century.

THE BUSINESS DATA STORE IS NOT A PROGRESSIVE PROGRAM TO STIFLE BUSINESS

The Business Data Store (BDS) is the property of the business. Like the PDS, the Business Data Store will help to improve government efficiency. Unlike the PDS however, the cost of the BDS is entirely borne by the business without government funding. In fact, the BDS reduces the government costs in data storage.

The added costs businesses have in maintaining a BDS is offset in several ways. Businesses can now understand better what data the government requires. Secondly, government can be assured that the data is pertaining to the business. Both groups can be sure that the data is accessed appropriately.

THE FEDERAL LOCAL MAGISTRATE COURT IS NOT A PROGRESSIVE PROGRAM

The FLMC provides a way to resolve issues at a more local level. The FLMC also provides a way to reduce the reach of the federal government.

Cases heard before the FLMC include what is called administrative law. These cases are currently heard in courts which are part of the executive branch. These types of cases, have for the most part devolved to where it is necessary to have specialized attorneys to hear the cases, and where the tendency to "tilt" in favor of the government is clear simply from the length of time most of these cases tend to be cleared. That delay is ALWAYS in the favor of the government.

The second kind of case is in the area of civil rights. These cases usually include trying to find the "deep pockets" to sue. This has caused the largest number of cases simply to be ignored. This also is because of the tendency to have attorneys hear the cases. The creation of the FLMC is actually a counterbalance to this longstanding direction of government to be increasingly expansive.

THE FEDERAL INFORMATION SERVICE AND THE NEW FEDERAL PROJECTS ARE NOT JUST MORE GOVERNMENT

Every single attempt to reduce the size of the executive branch of the government by eliminating departments even at cabinet levels has simply resulted in more government being created. That is why the Federal Information Service is a creature of the legislative branch. The projects and programs being reviewed and the actions being taken can be really summarized in just a few simple goals for the entire FIS.

- Stand up the FNO throughout the United States.

- Stand up the FLMC throughout the US.

- Set up the support structures for these new delivery mechanisms.

- Ensure that the procedures are clear for the FNO and FLMC.

- Eliminate redundant services by different federal agencies.

- Revise old support structures and when duplicated services are found to eliminate the old support structures through recommendations to the Congress.

Basically the entire purpose of the FIS is to both reduce the size of the centralized federal government AND to improve the performance of the decentralized Federal Government.

CONCLUSION

There is no hidden agenda for this book. If you find you agree with enough of what this book is about to want to know more, or even better participate, please visit the websites listed in Chapter 16 for more information. If you would like to suggest I include your perspective in upcoming books, please email me at Steve@SteveImholt.com.

GOV. 2.0 – A PROGRESSIVE PERSPECTIVE

The entire book is really about how to merge some of the demands of conservatives into a coherent approach. It is not simply to surrender to those demands. The approach itself has an underlying goal of reforming the structure. This will help the American people to regain control of the operations of the government.

In the last century the role of the federal government has grown in ways both intended and unintended. The result is people no longer can have a direct effect on the performance of the government. The book as a whole is the beginning of a road map of how to regain that control. Even better, it does it in a controlled fashion.

Through the rejuvenation of neighborhoods, communities can better control their neighborhoods. They can regain responsibility for the performance of the federal government within those neighborhoods. These results can be profound in all the ways that are most important.

The result of these actions is that local control of how services are delivered will again be possible. This is true even though the programs and procedures are federal in nature. And that local control will cut the higher costs of central administration. This makes more funds available for local use. This reduces the power of the bureaucracy to cripple the rights of the individual.

Moving the services to the FNOs means that the contracting model will be small. Large corporations will no longer dominate the executive branch. In that way their influence will be significantly reduced. And what's more, the local FNO board helps insure that people get government services more fairly.

The creation of the Federal Local Magistrate Court helps to protect people's rights much better than today. The FLMC will improve the processes to assure the people's rights are protected. Today, core rights are often denied because of the long processes required. The FLMC can now address those issues more rapidly. Through these improved processes, the stated demands of the conservatives can be met while in actuality not surrendering to those demands.

Some progressives will still claim that Gov 2.0 is anything but an acceptable approach to improve government. They will say that none of it is acceptable to a "real" progressive. For those people, the following sections provide another view of the major components.

THE FEDERAL NEIGHBORHOOD OFFICE IS NOT A CONSERVATIVE TRICK

Some of the most important aspects of Gov 2.0 have two counter balanced objectives. For example, the FNO has one objective to more effectively deliver federal services. These services comprise a large piece of the Federal Budget. The FNO moves the delivery of those services to a smaller local level.

As services are moved to the FNOs, duplicate services are eliminated from the old federal system. This reduces the cost of operations.

LETTING ENTREPRENEURSHIP THRIVE

The FNO board is selected by local community. FNO operations are mostly done by local businesses selected by the FNO board. This lets the FNO board decide if they want to support small businesses, which is very likely. This then allows those small businesses to compete against larger companies in providing services to the residents. This reduces the influence of big business.

Even better, local businesses tend to hire people from the local community. This way communities share in the revenues of the federal government.

RESTORING CIVIC PARTICIPATION

The FNO board provides a chance for communities to be involved in government. This helps the local community to take responsibility for the growth and survival of each community across the country. This is in stark contrast to the Federal Executive Branch which tends to ignore local community input.

The FNOs are not an endorsement or critique of any specific service. That is for discussions between progressives and conservatives. But local FNOs are not expected to over reach on government programs as much as happens today.

There will however be one result at the local level that should be welcomed. The impact of conservative self-appointed champions of the people should be reduced.

THE PERSONAL DATA STORE IS NOT A BIG BUSINESS POWER GRAB

The data that the government has about a person was always held by independent government agencies. Now as agencies integrate their information stores that your information becomes increasingly subject to government scrutiny. The ability to merge that data is rapidly growing. Now government can get a detailed picture of where you are in your life. Today, government has more data about you than it does about most foreign heads of state.

Prior to the information age, there really was no alternative. Today however, that does not have to be the case. Instead, your information should be more like an old style bankbook. The old style bankbook let you present it to the authorities, that is the bank. They would then perform their tasks (such as deposits and withdrawals). Now, instead of "presenting" your bankbook, the government has to "request" your information from your "banker". In this case the "banker" is your PDS vendor. In turn the PDS vendor has to record the access, the purpose of the access, the agency or GAA who requested the access, and what information they retrieved. In most ways this is tremendously more control of the individual and their information than even the most conservative groups have requested.

The government will keep your data from now on unless something dramatic happens. There appear to be no plans to shut down Social Security. The same is true of Medicare, and the IRS. Each of these programs has your information. And you have no idea who is accessing it. But at least with the PDS approach, you can tell when your information is being accessed, and at least in theory tell what the reason was for the access. This also is a huge improvement on the current environment from just about everyone's point of view, where now you have no idea whether your information is being accessed for good or for ill.

The book references companies like Yahoo, Google, IBM, and HP in a number of places. This may give the idea that only large vendors are able to provide a PDS. Actually, any qualified network, software or technology company can provide that ability. This could even include some which would be local.

THE FEDERAL ID CARD IS A NECESSARY TOOL

Some conservatives believe that some people today take advantage of the system. They believe this happens in a number of ways. One way is through being paid for duplicated services. Another way is when a person defrauds the system using fake or duplicated IDs. They believe it also happens where eligibility is separated from the distribution of funds. The Federal ID Card helps to reduce fraud by making it mandatory to get federal services.

That same thinking applies to a person voting multiple times in a single election. The use of a Federal ID card would clearly eliminate that problem.

It really is the same idea as the original Social Security card. Everyone received a card with a unique Social Security Number. This is taking that idea and extending it to the 21st century.

THE BUSINESS DATA STORE IS NOT A CONSERVATIVE WAY TO FAVOR BUSINESSES

The Business Data Store (BDS) is the property of the business. Like the PDS, the Business Data Store will help to improve government efficiency. Unlike the PDS however, the cost of the BDS is entirely borne by the business without government funding. In fact, the BDS reduces the government costs in data storage.

The added costs businesses have in maintaining a BDS is offset in several ways. Businesses can now understand better what data the government requires. Secondly, government can be assured that the data is pertaining to the business. Both groups can be sure that the data is accessed appropriately.

THE FEDERAL LOCAL MAGISTRATE COURT IS NOT A WAY TO DENY PEOPLE'S RIGHTS

The FLMC provides a way to resolve issues at a more local level. The FLMC also provides a way to reduce the reach of the federal government.

Cases heard before the FLMC include what is called administrative law. These cases are currently heard in courts which are part of the executive branch. These types of cases, have for the most part devolved to where it is necessary to have specialized attorneys to hear the cases, and where the tendency to "tilt" in favor of the government is clear simply from the length of time most of these cases tend to be cleared. That delay is ALWAYS in the favor of the government.

The second kind of case is in the area of civil rights. These cases usually include trying to find the "deep pockets" to sue. This has caused the largest number of cases simply to be ignored. This also is because of the tendency to have attorneys hear the cases. The creation of the FLMC is actually a counterbalance to this longstanding direction of government to be increasingly expansive.

THE FEDERAL INFORMATION SERVICE AND THE NEW FEDERAL PROJECTS ARE NOT GOING TO ELIMINATE SERVICES

The FIS is described and designed to reduce the inefficiencies in government NOT to eliminate functions within the executive branch. Adding new programs, or eliminating existing programs, remains the responsibility of the legislative and executive branches through the same mechanisms currently in place. That is why the Federal Information Service is a creature of the legislative branch. The projects and programs being reviewed and the actions being taken can be really summarized in just a few simple goals for the entire FIS.

- Stand up the FNO throughout the United Stated.

- Stand up the FLMC throughout the US.

- Set up the support structures for these new delivery mechanisms.

- Ensure that the procedures are clear for the FNO and FLMC.

- Eliminate redundant services by different federal agencies.

- Revise old support structures and only where duplicated eliminate the old support structures through recommendations to the Congress.

Basically the entire purpose of the FIS is to both reduce the size of the federal government AND to improve the performance of the Federal Government.

GOV 2.0 – LIBERTARIAN PERSPECTIVE

This book is about reforming government. A pure libertarian would claim that all government inherently reduces the freedoms that all people so any book that reduces the size of government is good. This book doesn't directly try to reduce the size of government. As a result, it is easy to claim that all libertarians should vehemently advocate against this book.

If you are a hard-core libertarian, you must agree that you are putting yourself into a difficult position. You need to get not only a majority of the people to agree with your position. You must also keep them in agreement long enough to root out those in power. That is especially true for those who want to retain power above all else.

Given the situation it seems that a purely libertarian government is unlikely within the next several national elections. Does that make your goal wrong? No. But it does mean that your goal is not a near term expectation.

So the questions are "Do the ideas and concepts in this book allow for the continued fostering of a more libertarian approach?" And "Does the book push the electorate to continue to support those who actually control the government?"

Clearly, the book does not support the status quo. The book doesn't support an expansion in the federal government. At worst the book reorganizes federal services into something more efficient. As overlaps in services are eliminated the size of government is reduced.

The expanded use of the private sector itself can be used to foster a more positive view of libertarianism. While this would be a slow process, I believe it will provide both a short-term goal. That goal in fact would be consistent with the longer-term goal.

The rest of the book should be viewed as a way to make government less corrupt. At least by making it less corrupt, the corruption can then be rooted our more easily.

If after this you still vehemently oppose the ideas within this book I suggest you read the a later perspective in this appendix, The Single Issue Individual Proponent Perspective.

GOV 2.0 – AN ACTIVE REPUBLICAN PERSPECTIVE

For years Republicans have tended to view any new federal program as bad. That's because each new program makes it easier to expand the reach of the federal government.

GOVERNMENT 2.0 IS NOT ONLY ABOUT MORE EFFECTIVE GOVERNMENT

For the moment, assume that Government 2.0 is different, at least while you read the remainder of the book. I suggest you keep reading. You should continue until you realize a liberal would never have actually described things to this ridiculous level of detail. Remember, that the actual numbers of government employees to be hired to implement Government 2.0 is under 25,000 people. This includes both the FIS and the related agencies. This increase is more than offset by an enormous amount of people being shifted off the public payroll. Instead, they will be part of the contracted services provided to the FNO by local companies.

The actual number of people I would expect to be moved to the civilian work force is likely to be in excess of 2 million people. This includes the 600,000 plus employees of the US Postal Service. Most people administering Social Security, the majority of personnel in Internal Revenue Service, and the other re-engineered agencies will no longer be part of the federal civil service. This means they also won't be receiving raises simply based on longevity, they. Government employees also won't continue to receive the extravagant benefit packages. This WILL reduce the size of government.

GOVERNMENT 2.0 IS NOT ONLY ABOUT A SMALLER GOVERNMENT

It has long been recognized by Republicans that there is no actual push towards real efficiencies in government. This has resulted in not only duplication of function, but functions which are intended to be inefficient to protect the jobs that the civil service and thus the employee unions control. Despite the protests of progressives and democrats who receive massive campaign contributions from people who work in the public sector that they are overworked, the reality is that while many public employees are convinced they are overworked, any claim they may have is far outweighed by the impact of those who game the system.

By transferring more responsibility for delivery to private companies, the government can regain what they are good at which is regulating private industry, and get out of the service delivery process where they have provide ample evidence of the complete inability of government to manage delivery in the long term.

GOVERNMENT 2.0 IS ABOUT MAKING GOVERNMENT WORK BETTER NOT ONLY LESS

In 1993 I worked on a system to dispose of hazardous material. The regulations at that time (coming out of a Republican administration) were over 1500 pages of fine print, some of which was almost indecipherable to any normal reading

One reason the EPA regulations were so difficult is that it was one of the easiest places to "hide things" in broad daylight. For example, at the time, any hazardous natural gas emissions, or pollution of waste water from a section of Chicago east of the Dan Ryan and South of the main city, was by the very legislation deemed not to be subject to be hazardous material laws and thus outside the bounds of the EPA. Co-incidentally this was an area where the industry effectively underwrote the career of Dan Rostenkowski. Even some of the EPA manuals described the exception as the Dan Rostenkowski exception, because of the clout of the that "renowned" democratic congressman.

In all honesty, most active citizens are aware of similar cases of excess or to use the blunt term, corruption within other agencies. About the only way out of that morass, is to have an independent set of eyes on each procedure, process, or function, report the inefficiency or excess, and then have that corruption be publicized in order to begin to address those problems.

THE PDS IS SAFER FOR YOUR DATA THAN THE GOVERNMENT SYSTEMS WILL EVER BE

Gov 2.0 will make the data in the individual PDS safer than if it's kept on multiple government servers, where if it is compromised, you may never even know it. Being blunt, there is no benefit to the agency to keeping your data safe, as long as the access by anyone is not publicized. Having your data under your control is at least as safe as having it under the government's control, and again being blunt, at least that way you know your information is safe FROM the eyes of the federal agency employee or contractor.

GOV 2.0 – AN ACTIVE DEMOCRAT PERSPECTIVE

It is likely that the actual creation of the Federal Neighborhood Office and the Federal Local Magistrate Courts will be viewed very positively by most active democrats.

It is at the staffing and service levels that some democrats will automatically object. The reality is, that because the services are being so standardized, the number of FNOs and FLMCs will force the staffing to be locally based whether through private contractors or through local staffing for larger contractors. Either way this provides a local economic stimulus for both the people working at the FNO, as well as the very real costs of setting up the physical facilities. This will be especially beneficial to the local communities so negatively impacted by the Great Recession. Further, because segmentation of the population into such discrete collections, will allow more effective delivery of government services.

While there are obvious advantages to being able to resolve civil liberty cases rapidly, there are likely going to be a number of concerns that the FLMC will never actually be implemented.

Adequate controls to insure that the FLMC is set up concurrently with the local FNO must be within any legislation, but assuming that is the case, it clearly is something that active democrats will agree is a clear societal benefit.

There are also two other areas of concern that some activists may also have. These are, the historical basis of local communities not always protecting rights of individuals, and given that history, some democrats may decide that the risks outweigh the potential benefit of actually enforcing equality of rights. This is a legitimate concern that can only be validated through the Proof of Concept and Pilot phases. But if that risk is found to be overcome, the benefits are very real and should be supported enthusiastically.

The other area of concern, is that by making the adjudication of the rights be directly taken at the local level, the "deep pocket" civil rights litigation cases will be much less common. In turn, that may affect some sources of funding for other liberal causes. But I believe most active democrats will also decide that in this case, actually succeeding in making equality of rights a reality is worth the loss of some funding.

GOV 2.0 – A GEEK PERSPECTIVE

For most hard-core geeks, the rather flippant lack of rigor on standard terms, the lack of clear bounds, the lack of peer review and most especially the lack of quality controls and documentation can only be met with a sincere apology.

This book at least through the draft revision stage has been done without funding, and obviously with little actual peer review. It is to be expected that there are gaps, errors and flawed logic when all of the above is true.

But from a strategic level, it is sufficient to engage our customer the public, in the summary levels that will follow this book.

If you find you agree with enough of what this book is about to want to know more, or even better participate, please visit the websites listed in Chapter 16 for more information.

GOV 2.0 – AN UNALIGNED VOTER PERSPECTIVE

Thank you for reading this book. As an independent voter who is actually interested in what this book is about, it's most likely that you are someone who is trying to figure out what the books purpose is.

Surprisingly, the books purpose is get people like you actually talking with all these other groups of geeks, wonks, republicans, democrats, liberals, conservative and yes even the low information voter. It is only through actually having real dialog that we have any hope of making this system work effectively again.

GOV 2.0 – A WONK PERSPECTIVE

It would be worthwhile if as a self-appointed policy geek, you actually did read the entirety of the book, but given the time constraints you all face, perhaps you can get enough through the stories, and the major components. You may have significant concerns about the practicality of implementing this kind of change in today's world. On a personal note, I do as well. I am not concerned if the changes aren't practical. Not am I concerned that the changes won't work as advertised. I'm much more concerned that wonks, politicians, and K street lobbyists are more concerned with retaining power in one form or another than actually succeeding in meeting any of their individually advertised goals.

So consider this perspective to be a challenge. The challenge for you as a wonk is to try to think like an architect and less like a wonk. If you wish to think of things from an architectural basis, when you see a gap, a weakness or a problem with an approach, a concept, or a component it is completely appropriate to describe the problem. BUT, in filling the role of architect you should also at least suggest a way for the problem to be eliminated, reduced, mitigated or avoided.

If you actually want to respond to that challenge, you may in addition to raising the problems in your writing, can you please also forward your observations to Steve@SteveImholt.com

GOV 2.0 – A PERSPECTIVE FOR THE SINGLE ISSUE READER

It is an unfortunate reality that both political parties and candidates include in their platforms positions on some issues only because it appeals to single issue voters. With hundreds of issues, the number of single-issue voters can actually swing elections. This is why candidates court those voters,

Whether the voter is totally committed to the 2nd Amendment (or totally opposed), totally committed to women's rights (or opposed), or any of hundreds of other issues, (including the rights of troglodytes), the voters realize that these commitments are solely to gain votes.

So when the ability to actually get coherent views from people within the district through the FNO local issue voting, views that really do represent the will of the people are actually more likely to be adopted, since candidates are not likely to support a position that won't gain any votes.

As a result, those who really do believe in a particular issue, must first convince the voters in a district at the local level. It is no longer be sufficient to push agendas through both public and hidden contributions to candidates. This can fundamentally change the ability of single issues to actually, finally be resolved at least for a period of time.

Barring this kind of alternative, we will continue to have our TV time interrupted by claims and accusations about candidates on issues about which most of us really don't care.

So even if the changes for Gov 2.0 don't actually support your issue, it's probably a good idea if only to be able to see what the next dumb used car commercial can appear next.

Nevertheless, if you really believe your single issue should be included somehow within Gov2.0, and you wish to participate please visit the websites listed in Chapter 16 for more information.

GOV 2.0 – LOW INFORMATION VOTER (LIV) PERSPECTIVE

All the important people know this is a great idea. So if you really are a LIV you have all you need to know.

But, if you've actually read this entire book, please admit to yourself, that you really aren't a Low Information Voter. So use one of your favorite pseudonyms and visit the web sites listed in Chapter 16.

APPENDIX D DETAILS ABOUT THE PDS

In effect the FDOSA is responsible for defining and maintaining the standards for the following:

APPROPRIATE INDIVIDUAL ACCESS

You must have the ability to access and maintain your information. At the same time, in order to access your information there must be some method to insure that you are the person accessing the information. This is one of the primary uses of the FIC Card. For the authorized FIC cardholder, a linkage to their PDS and the FIC card will always allow for access to the person's PDS. Once that linkage is established, the FIC and PDS can also be used **BY THE INDIVIDUAL** to identify those devices (cell phones, PCs, laptops etc.) which are to be considered safe accesses (that is not requiring the use of the FIC card to directly access the individuals PDS. FDOSA will be responsible for maintaining the technology standards for FIC cards, and PDS GAA vendors to insure that this access is appropriately used.

PDS VENDOR LICENSING

Vendors who can offer the Personal Data Stores will need to be federally licensed to maintain strict standards of confidentiality, and security, especially FROM the government as well as securing things for individuals for access by individuals. These will be among the first GAAs of Government 2.0. PDS GAA vendors must fully support each person's ability to move his Personal Data Store from vendor to vendor.

PDS PRICING

Vendors will negotiate prices with the government for the basic service, and based on that standard service, individual PSA owners are expected to pay for any services beyond that minimum.

REASONABLE INFORMATION REQUIREMENTS OF FEDERAL AND STAGE AGENCIES FOR KEEPING ABOUT THE INDIVIDUAL WHICH IS NOT WITHIN THE INDIVIDUAL PDS

The reasonable amount of information that the government would need to retain about you as a citizen would be a minimal set of demographic data. This would include Security Keys for particular sets of government data, for example a separate key for use by the IRS to get at your IRS data, a separate key for your Social Security data for use by the Social Security Administration.

Beyond those keys the general information retained at each agency should be:

- Your name
- Your social security number
- Your physical address

- Your electronic address (where your PDS is stored under your control).

Note that your electronic address forms the basis for the record in the Personal Data Store Network described in Chapter 2.

TYING GOVERNMENT ACCESS TO YOUR RIGHT TO KNOW

The government needs to have the ability to access your information but generally it doesn't have the authority to do so **anonymously**. It does have the ability to retrieve your information in order to perform a legitimate governmental function, and the **responsibility to report to you** when that information has been retrieved. For that reason every government access to your PDS is recorded in the PDS itself, and by the vendor.

Accesses to your information by staff of the PDS Vendor or an agent of the federal government beyond those necessary to perform an authorized government function will through legislation be considered a civil rights crime with penalties up to and including prison and fines.

GOVERNMENT INSTITUTIONAL VIOLATIONS

Government institutional violations of privacy are those where any person in a position of authority accesses, or directs others to access an individual's information for any purpose beyond that necessary to perform a legitimate government function.

Governmental institutional violations of privacy is no less a crime and intentional inappropriate accesses of individuals information at the direction of management within an agency must also treated as a crime with the same levels of penalty for both managers and the individual actually violating the law. It should also result in the penalties including termination of the person or persons providing the direction to access the information illegally as well as the individuals who actually execute those directions.

VENDOR INSTITUTIONAL VIOLATIONS

For PDS vendors inappropriate accesses of individual's information as a result of directions within the PDS Vendor organization, is no different that government institutional crime, with the same penalties for the person or persons issuing the directions as those who actually execute those directions. In addition, for vendors, there can also be civil rights penalties and fines, if the vendor's policies and procedures either condone, or allow such activities.

PRIVACY VIOLATION PENALTIES

Make the penalty for illegal retrieval of personal information a new type of federal crime, with the first court of law for these charges being the new community courts.

Make conviction of a crime for illegal access or retrieval of information from an individual's Personal Data Store be considered as an individual rights violation. Don't treat it as a matter of theft only when it involves financial data. Repeat offenses should be dealt with in the same fashion as repeat offenders in every way. Offenses up to and including multiple years in incarceration should be set up as an established appropriate penalty set.

GAA AND GOVERNMENT HACKING

Additionally certain categories of employment by definition must be of the highest level of integrity. When these standards of integrity are abused, heavier penalties must be used in order to restore public confidence in both government and any companies involved in that breach of trust.

ROGUE GOVERNMENT HACKING

Individuals in the employ of the US government who intentionally retrieve or are provided with individual information which is not specifically authorized or even if authorized is used in an unauthorized manner are subject to penalties with an increased level of severity.

That is, a first offense by someone working for the IRS who access the information without authorization is at a minimum deserve to have the same rules applied more stringently, so that first time offenses automatically be charged at level in the same way as a repeat offender within the general citizenry. In addition,

.

- Federal employees, who are convicted of this type of offense, are precluded from being hired by any agency of the federal government.

- Federal employees who are convicted of this type of crime, should lose all accrued pension benefits

DIRECTED GOVERNMENTAL ROGUE HACKING

When a federal employee has been directed by a supervisor or manager to knowingly engage in inappropriate accessing of an individual's personal information, both the manager and the actual actor are equally at fault, and should be prosecuted commensurate with that fault.

GAA ROGUE HACKING

Employees of GAAs are also in a position of public trust. As such the penalties for repeat offenders are applied to first offenses by employees of GAA vendors, except for the loss of pension. They will also be barred from future federal employment.

DIRECTED GAA ROGUE HACKING

As with the government sector, supervisors who direct employees to hack are just as guilty as the government sector supervisor.

EXCEPTIONS TO THE CONTROLLED ACCESS

A search warrant must always be issued in order for the government to access your information. This is true even in National Security cases. Only then can your vendor allow your information to be accessed without telling you right away. How long your information can be accessed without telling you must be in the warrant. Once the warrant has expired, your logging functions will notify you that your information has been accessed. The only way that you will not be told is if the search warrant is changed to continue the surveillance.

As mentioned before when a person cannot handle their own affairs, they may grant this to another person as a guardian. The courts may act in the same way. Courts may also appoint a guardian when a person has been judged to be incompetent. When that happens, the guardian is given access with specific authorities when granted by an appropriate court.

HOW CAN A NORMAL CITIZEN REALLY KNOW THAT THEIR INFORMATION IS SECURE FROM THE GOVERNMENT

Every month every approved vendor must provide the stats on how many individual PDSs they maintain were subjected to searches. This would include both standard court order and national security court orders. This information would need to include at least the percentage or court orders for the total PDS individuals the vendor supports, along with how many individual PDS were notified that they had been accessed through a search warrant.

HOW CAN AN ORDINARY CITIZEN REALLY KNOW THEIR INFORMATION IS SECURE FROM HACKING?

Along with the statistics on government search warrants, the vendors must provide a count of how many attempts were made to "hack" into the PDS systems. This would include a count of how many attempts appear to have been successful. This information would need to be provided both for the preceding month but also prior months as a whole to provide a standard for comparison. While no system can be considered fully secure, this information should allow the owner to decide if the services provided to you by the vendor are sufficient.

HOW SECURE DO YOU WANT YOUR ACCESS TO BE?

In order to get into your PDS the first time, you must have a Federal ID Card. You must also use it at one of the new Federal Neighborhood Offices, or at a local Post Office who provides the service. You could also use one of the State DMV or at a Social Security office.

With your Federal ID Card, you can log into your PDS at any federal office that has a card reader. The first time you do so, you can access an initial set of information. During that first access, you also select which vendor you want to use. You can also identify if you want to be able to get into your PDS without actually using your FIC. You could for example set up your home computer to access your PDS even if it does not have a card reader. You do that by creating a security ID for your home computer, and then use it

along with your credentials from that computer along
with a user name and a password.

You could also buy a card reader for use at home,
which would then provide the same protection you
would receive at any FNO.

Since part of your card is machine readable, you could
use a smartphone to access your PDS as well. That can
be done using either a secure reader or a digital
fingerprint.

The specific criteria to be used, depends on your PDS
vendor. It also depends on which level of security you
need (and which you are willing to pay for to your PDS
vendor). How much security you need is your decision.

WHO PAYS FOR THIS?

The federal government will pay for part of the cost of
the government wing for each PDS owner. Beyond that
cost, vendors may charge for the rest of the PDS.
Generally, people pay for their personal folders. People
would also have to pay for additional services such as
enhanced security and backup of personal folders.

APPENDIX E DETAILS OF THE FLMC

FLMC CASE ADMINISTRATION

The FLMC has both limited jurisdiction and powers. The types of cases, the venue and rules of evidence are simplified to provide a rapid, yet intrinsically fairer trial.

The normal sequence of a case is as follows when the case is brought by an individual:

FILING A CASE

All cases must be filed in the FNO by the person making the charge. Since the FLMC and the FNO are primarily service locations, there is no support locally for most of the trappings of larger courts. Filing is done online. It is submitted through the FNO portal and directed to the Chief Magistrate[26] for the local FLMC.

ROUTING OF CASES

Based on the complaint, the Chief Magistrate has one of three basic options to deal with the case.

FLMC APPROPRIATE CASES

If the case is for either a federal misdemeanor complaint, or a civil rights complaint against an

---

26 The Chief Magistrate is one of the Federal Local Magistrates selected by the member magistrates of the FLMC itself. More details are contained below

individual, the case will be handled initially through the FLMC.

1) DISTRICT ATTORNEY CASES

If the case appears to be a felony case or is beyond the scope of the FLMC in any way, the case is directed to the US States Attorney for the local District. The local district attorney may also set local rules by which the Chief Magistrate may direct the case to the District Magistrate for administration of the complaint.

2) INCOMPLETE COMPLAINTS

For those complaints which are such that it cannot be determined what is the appropriate direction for the case the Chief Magistrate will contact the complainant to clarify the complaint in order to appropriately direct the case.

NORMAL FLMC CASE PROCESSING

Because the FLMC is intended to be a LOCAL federal court and due to the elected nature of the magistrates elected to administer the FLMC, the court is a limited extension of the federal system to adjudicate cases. As a result, many of the standard rules and procedures are simplified to make the administration both streamlined, and suitable to task.

RULINGS AND IMPACTS

The court is further limited in that it can only come out with rulings that fall within predefined guidelines. The

following are the rulings that a case can appropriately
be resolved in

- No Grounds which can be due to there
  being no legitimate grounds for the suit, in
  which case the plaintiff pays for the court
  costs as well as the cost of any attorneys
  involved.
- No Grounds because the charges can be
  legitimately made in state court, which
  means that each party pays its own costs.
- Not Guilty (where the plaintiff pays the
  cost of the court and any attorneys
  involved).
- Guilty but no recompense where the
  defendant is found guilty but each party
  pays for their own attorneys (if any) and
  the court costs are split evenly
- Guilty, where the defendant pays for the
  court and their own attorney costs up to
  $5,000
- Presumed Felony where the severity of the
  offense is significant and the defendant
  has a probability of being guilty. This
  finding does not carry a guilty verdict until
  the case is adjudicated at the Federal
  Circuit court level.

APPEALS

Verdicts that result in any of the various forms of guilty
can be appealed by the defendant. The appeal would
need to be made to the district court magistrate.

When the complaint is a civil case, and the defendant is found not responsible, the verdict may also be appealed. In that case, the costs of the appeal must be borne entirely by the plaintiff. The appeal is made to the district court magistrate.

SHARED MAGISTRATES

Because people do not all live in the same FNO when a case if brought against an individual who is a resident anywhere but within the local FNO service area, the FNO of the defendant is contacted and the magistrate from the defendant's local FNO will be able to participate as an observer. Other rules for appeals will occur in those cases, but basically, on guilty verdict, the appeal will be to the District Court Magistrate of the Defendant's Federal Court District, and appeals of Not Guilty will be appealed to the plaintiff's Federal District Court magistrate of the plaintiff.

ROLE OF THE LOCAL MAGISTRATE (FLMC)

Each FLMC has one Federal Local Magistrate per FNO that comprises the FLMC territory. The Federal Local Magistrate has relatively broad powers in determining what level of offense needs to be directed to the Federal Circuit Courts. By having a local magistrate, they are better able to determine whether the need to move over to the rest of the Federal Court system is in the best interests of the community, as well as the plaintiff and defendant.

INITIAL APPOINTMENT FOR NEW FNO'S

When a new FNO is being opened, the Federal Local Magistrate for the FNO is appointed by the corresponding Federal District Magistrate Judge who will be receiving referred cases, and will be the first level of appeal for cases appealed from the FLMC.

TERM OF THE FLM

Each elected term of the FLM is for four years, and no FLM may serve more than two consecutive terms unless the local FNO approves a continuation by local FNO vote referendum.

QUALIFICATIONS OF A FLM

Each FLM must be a registered voter, a resident of the FNO to which they are appointed, not currently under parole or confinement for state or local felony, and must complete a mandatory training within 90 days of appointment. It is expected that this training will be no more than 80 hours that will be paid for by the government both for the cost of the training and the time of the FLM.

FLM CHIEF MAGISTRATE

Each FLMC has a chief magistrate elected by the magistrates of the FLMC on the first Monday after the quadrennial election.

FLM REMUNERATION

Each FLM is remunerated at the rate of $20 per hour except for the Chief Magistrate of the FLMC, which shall be remunerated at the rate of $25 per hour, unless adjusted by act of Congress upon recommendation of the Federal Judiciary.

DUTIES OF CHIEF MAGISTRATE

The Chief Magistrate, in addition to having the duties of the magistrate is responsible for the assignment of cases to the magistrates within the FLMC. In addition, for cases brought by residents of another FLMC jurisdiction against residents within the FLMC jurisdiction, the Chief Magistrate may assign a magistrate as observer within the other FLMC court.

ABOUT THE AUTHOR

Steve Imholt is a long time project manager, IT architect, designer and developer. Steve has been both witness and part of the evolution of the Information Age. He has worked with computers since the days of punched cards and designed services to operate within the cloud.

Steve has had a front line view of the evolution of technology.

In the 1970's Steve gained his initial experiences in healthcare as a systems engineer trainee at EDS. This was the time where the Medicare processing expansion hit its stride. This was followed by a short time where he worked at Merchant's National Bank. It was here where he helped implement the banks first interest bearing checking accounts. This was followed by a period where Steve was the DP manager for a grocery store chain just as Universal Product Codes were being introduced to the grocery industry.

In the 1980's Steve gained even more experience in the health care field in both hospitals and insurers. This was a time where there were rapid changes in health insurance. New concepts such as HMOs and PPOs were added by insurance companies. New frameworks such as Certificates of Need and health networks were added. These were all failed attempts to get health care costs under control.

It was during this time that Steve dabbled in local politics being elected to a local school board. There he served as co-chair of the finance committee. After moving because of job changes, Steve then served on a community library board. Steve developed a better understanding of political groups because of these experiences. He also saw how politics was very different between the levels of government. Steve saw how special interest groups of all types were beginning to affect all the layers of government.

Technology in the 1980s and 90s was the age of the Client Server world. Along with companies like HP and Compac, Steve's skills changed to be a force within that world. In that world, he learned about the real complexities of safely disposing of hazardous materials. He also learned about the pork barrel regulations. Regulations such as excluding sites where Congress received large contributions. It was these kinds of regulations that blocked moves to clean up some parts of the environment. That was the Environmental Protection Agency of the time. Sadly, it is also the EPA of today, simply with a different set of special interests.

In the mid-90s allowed Steve was asked to manage the development of a mortgage loan origination system. These loans were for manufactured housing, which most people call mobile homes. The origination system was a way for a REIT[27] to create Securities. Because mobile home loans usually were less than high quality,

---

27 REIT stands for Real Estate Investment Trust. These were companies specifically set up to create Mortgage Backed Securities, which fueled the investment expansion of the 1990s and early 2000s.

they became part of the Subprime Mortgage Loan market. It was these types of Securities many people blame as a major cause of the Great Recession.

From there after failing at starting his own IT business, Steve became a software Architect. He took that role beginning in the summer of 2001 working for Tauck which is the world's oldest group travel company. They were located outside of New York City in Westport Connecticut. Like many others Tauck was devastated by 9/11. In the course of two weeks, that company like others saw the size of its business drop in half. Steve was fortunate enough to be able to continue working with them until 2003. At that time, the company could no longer support the size and scope of their re-engineering efforts. As a result, they offered and Steve took a retirement package.

Finally in the early 2004's Steve began work with Hewlett Packard on the New York City ECTP program. ECTP was a NYC program to update the city's emergency response systems. There Steve learned about the bid and development processes used by government agencies. Those same processes were seen during his time at the United States Postal Service Project. As Steve helped an old friend bid on a Veterans administration project he learned that these processes were not unique to HP. Instead the processes for both bids and development are dictated by the government rules.

Multiple HP projects followed. While a few dealt with the commercial sectors, most projects continued to be in government. Some were in national defense or hospitals. Other projects were in state government and education. As Steve's experiences proved increasingly valuable, Steve provided trouble-shooting support for several HP projects. These projects were generally those which were part of acquired companies. After the acquisition was completed was when the troubles became obvious. In most of these situations, at least part of the source of the trouble was in the flawed bid and project award processes themselves. In others it was the demand that changes have little or no effect on existing processes. The common thread was that all of these projects were inconsistent in the requirements and the solutions, in large part because of the bid and development processes.

All of these projects led him to the conclusion that the development process was no different between state and federal government. This was unfortunate, because these processes do not work.

Steve as an architect began looking for the real core issues confronting integrating technology with government. Why government systems are so difficult to successfully change or replace? Can the public in concert with business deliver a better way for technology to assist government?

All of these experiences directly lead to this series of books.

Steve lives in Richmond Virginia with his wife Toni. Together, they raised three girls and a boy. Their children are now adults with successful careers in their own right. One has a career in technology. Another has a career in education, A third is a pediatrician, and the fourth is an attorney.

Now Steve makes woefully inadequate attempts to help mentor three of the four granddaughters. The reality is success is a result of his wife mentoring, cuddling and teaching the next generation as the preeminent grandma at our home now accurately renamed Gram's House.